C000108442

Since retirement, Patti Trickett and her husband have pursued their favourite pastime of walking and sightseeing in England and abroad, particularly on the beautiful island of Crete and bought their pretty villa in the foothills of the Psiloritis Mountains. Living in their villa for six months of the year, they walked in the mountains and villages, explored the beautiful gorges and visited many historical sites, as well as helping their Cretan friends to plant and harvest crops and cut grapes on the sunny slopes in the N.W. region. They have enjoyed so many unique experiences the average tourist never sees. This is a happy, light-hearted book which makes you smile!

This book is dedicated to the proud people of Crete…

Patti Trickett

Two Old Farts, Boots, Map and Compass

AUSTIN MACAULEY PUBLISHERS™

LONDON * CAMBRIDGE * NEW YORK * SHARJAH

A CIP catalogue record for this title is available from the British Library.

ISBN 9781398441545 (Paperback)
ISBN 9781398441552 (ePub e-book)

www.austinmacauley.com

First Published 2022
Austin Macauley Publishers Ltd®
1 Canada Square
Canary Wharf
London
E14 5AA

Walking and Adventures in England and Crete

We first became ambassadors of Crete, Greece, when we visited Agias Nicholias some 35 years ago on the recommendation of a Greek friend, in time to celebrate their Greek Easter.

We were very impressed with everything Crete had to offer, from being the warmest and friendliest people we know to their culture, their exquisite food and wine, their wide-ranging archaeology, and their long colourful history. All this left a deep imprint on us, and when we visited other places, we would always return to our beloved Crete.

The best thing we ever did was buying a little villa in the beautiful foothills of the Psiloritis Mountains near Rethymnon, there we made many loyal and loving friends and we have met many colourful characters whilst out walking and exploring the island. We feel very honoured and privileged to have witnessed a Cretan Baptism, partied in mountain villages, witnessed the locals shooting guns in the air, as part of their traditional celebrations, been invited to many Cretan Birthdays, Naming Days and Christmases, learnt some Greek dancing with our friends and had many wonderful BBQ's and watched the magnificent sunsets over the mountains and the sea. We picked grapes on a remote Cretan hillside and tread the juicy grapes with our bare feet in a big stone trough to make their beautiful Arcadi wine. We became a pair of hippies one summer, partying on the beautiful beach of Matala and dancing to live music at the festival. We think we have been very lucky to experience and share with you, The Real Crete!

Walking

AN EXTRACT FROM A POEM BY THOMAS TRAHERNE

1637–1674

To walk abroad is, not with eyes,
But thoughts, the fields to see and prize:
Else may the silent feet,
Like logs of wood,
Move up and down, and see no good
Nor joy nor glory meet.

***

To walk is by a thought to go;
To move in spirit to and fro;
To mind the good we see;
To taste the sweet;
Observing all the things we meet
How choice and rich they be.

***

To note the beauty of the day,
And golden fields of corn survey;
Admire each pretty flow'r
With its sweet smell;
To praise their Maker, and to tell, the marks of his great pow'r.

Chapter One
An Introduction

"THAT'S IT!" I declared, leaning back in my chair and grinning like a Cheshire Cat. "I have finished writing my first book." I looked over my shoulder at Chris, my husband, who had walked into the room. The back bedroom had been made over into an office so I could use the laptop and type my manuscript.

I had ventured into the relatively unknown world of writing, all about our travelling adventures in a motorhome which took us through central Europe in 2010/11. For the last two years, writing *Two Old Farts and a Motorhome* had taken over my life. I used a hand-held tape recorder to make notes when we were out walking and sightseeing in France, Switzerland, Germany, Italy, the Greek mainland, and Crete.

It took us nearly two years of planning the route we would take, booking ferries, booking campsites, and packing everything we thought we might need.

"It's not as easy as you think, disappearing for a few months."

We booked an overnight ferry with Anek Lines, excellent service, good food, and clean accommodation travelling from Hull to Rotterdam, starting our journey on September 1, 2011. We arrived early the next morning and drove out to find a lovely campsite for a couple of days in a pretty traditional village in Germany. There was a traditional German wine-fest in the village for a few days whilst we were there, which was really good fun. We did some walking through the beautiful vineyards situated around the sloping hillsides. Climbing out of the village to the very top, we looked across to a massive sea of pine trees in the Black Forest far beyond and in the distance, the magnificent Swabian Alps.

The next stop was to visit our family in Switzerland on the Swiss/German border and stay for ten days and did some walking whilst we were there. Our son took us on some lovely walks through the large pine forests near his home. Another day we all went up in a cable car to the very top of the Alps then did a few hours walking back down through the beautiful meadows, where pretty moo-eyed cows with large bells around their necks came to check us out.

Setting off again, we said goodbye to our family and drove over the beautiful Alps before heading towards the North East coast of Italy with golden sands and the blue sea of the Adriatic. We became a pair of hippy dropouts for a while, beachcombing for shells and collecting driftwood for a BBQ in the evenings. Sometimes we would only move Sapphire (our motorhome) a few kilometres further down the beach. We were enjoying the peace and tranquility it brought, now devoid of tourists, and being late September the weather was still lovely and the sea very warm from the summer sunshine.

Chris wanted to show me the Acropolis in Athens, so that was our next destination. We managed to find a nice campsite just outside Athens and over the road from a regular bus service. We stayed on the site for three days that time and did a lot of walking around the Acropolis itself as well as walking around the City and visiting places of interest.

Leaving Athens on mainland Greece, we were now heading down to the port of Piraeus to catch another ferry already booked to leave in two days. We drove into Korinthos town as the heavens opened and onto the marina car park to watch the rain. Putting on our waterproof coats, boots, and leggings, we braved the rain and found a coffee shop until we had decided what to do. The decision was taken out of our hands because when we returned to our motorhome there was a soggy bit of paper on the windscreen. It was advertising a new campsite not far from here and if we rang this number someone will come and escort us there.

"Sounds good to me," Chris said, smiling as he reached for the phone. These lovely people were as good as their word, and soon we were on electric hook up, warm and dry. Then there was a knock on the van door, it was the lovely old man holding a large umbrella in one hand and a tray of hot food in the other. We were thoroughly spoilt whilst we were there, and luckily the new site was situated near enough to walk to Ancient Corinth and enjoy all the beautiful archaeology. The morning we were leaving, the old man came across and gave us a big bag of oranges from his orchard as well as his homemade wine, handshakes and hugs, followed by the promise to come and visit the family.

We made excellent time at our next port of call to be ferried over to Chania, Crete, we had booked ahead with Anek Lines, and once again, we were impressed by their service. Arriving in the port of Chania, we drove our motorhome onto the main highway of Crete and arrived at our villa early evening to settle in and begin our winter holiday until February the following year.

Beetham Village – Circular Walk – 8 KMS

January has flown by, and we are into February already. As I write, I am happy to see the early morning sun peep through the grey wintery clouds. Now the days grow longer and the cold frosty mornings appear, it helps many keen walkers like ourselves to enjoy the lovely hills and dales of England and our beautiful countryside.

We have managed to get a few good walks this winter once the heavy rain had ceased for a while, giving some respite to the day. Large clusters of wild snowdrops line the route as we clump along in our heavy walking boots and gaiters along with layers of thick clothing and waterproofs. It's a wonder we can move at all!

I look closer at the waxy heads of the snowdrops, so perfectly formed and bobbing gently in the icy January air. It is one of the miracles of nature, hardy and resilient, and a sure sign that spring is well and truly on its way.

During the last few days of February, we have been blessed with some cold frosty nights with clear skies displaying a myriad of bright twinkling stars in a dark velvet sky. Early morning has brought warm sunshine and clear blue skies. We took advantage of excellent walking weather with the frozen ground making it easier to walk on instead of fields and lanes being a sodden messy bog and rivers and fords becoming impassable in parts.

On such a morning as this, when the sky was bright with winter sunshine, and the day was clear and dry we decided to get out early and do a walk. Whilst waiting for the sun to warm the chilly morning air a little, we filled a flask of coffee and made a sandwich for a picnic later. We have been rambling and walking for many years now, vigilant with regard to all the equipment we need to carry with us in our rucksacks.

Therefore, we packed our waterproof trousers, walks book, map, compass, first aid kit, torch and of course, boots. Our mobile phone is tucked away and turned off.

Our walk starts from The Wheatsheaf Hotel in the pretty village of Beetham, which is just off the A6, about five miles north of Carnforth, an hour's drive from our home on the Fylde Coast. It is a circular walk of eight kms. And just enough for a winter's afternoon when it goes dark early. Boots and gaiters on, waterproof coats on over thick jumpers, hats, gloves, and rucksacks, we set off mid-morning.

Walking past a few old stone cottages in the village, some gardens had large clusters of snowdrops and early crocus. These delicate crocuses reminded us of the magnificent display in the village churchyard at Poulton, Lancashire, planted many years ago. It has a colourful carpet of yellow, white and purple; it is well photographed and admired every year.

We reached a gate and walked into a large undulating field at the top end of the village, stopping to look at the lovely fourteenth-century Beetham Hall, still occupied and a busy working farm. One part of the Hall at the far end appears to be in a derelict state; it is still very beautiful and has an unusual structure with ornately carved windows. The Hall must have looked impressive when it was newly built all those years ago.

We were walking on The Limestone Link now; we were admiring many beautiful limestone rocks blanketed with thick emerald green mosses and lichen. Further along, we crossed a stone stile and just below us an opening into the small leafy woodland.

Walking along a quiet narrow lane, we came to a charming little shrine dedicated to St Liobia, an eighth-century Saxon Saint, dressed in her blue Benedictine habit and placed behind an old iron gate. Peering into the gloom we heard a constant drip of water leaching out of the porous rock above her head. Beetham church was originally dedicated to her, but after the Norman Conquest the church was re-named St Michael and All Angels. She is demoted to history now but still fondly thought of by the local people.

Continuing along in the warm winter sunshine, we walk between two walls passing by the charmingly named Fairy Steps Cottage to discover later that there is an actual place nearby, which we will do another day. We are now entering a beautiful wood, and all we can hear is our boots crunching along on the stony path along with decaying leaves and branches. The sun rays throw light and shadow through the tall thin trees, stripped bare of their autumn adornment. Many more naked branches lie rotting on the woodland floor, a natural habitat for all woodland creatures providing shelter.

Only an occasional cluster of snowdrops break a somewhat bleak winter landscape so typical of a midwinter scene. We were enjoying the walk through the clearly marked paths in the obviously 'managed' woodland. We came across our first purpose-built cairn pointing us to several alternative paths, coupled with well-placed and clearly marked signposts. Cheerful birdsong echoed around the otherwise silent woodland from a variety of birds high in the treetops, hopefully attracting a mate in the forthcoming spring.

The path turned onto a deeply rutted track, frozen hard with slivers of icy water, leaving some deep imprints from the soles of walking boots and dog paws, from when the paths were thick with mud during the heavy rain. We had to pick our way carefully over the rutted mounds of frozen soil to avoid stumbling and falling onto the hard ground. I amused myself by looking at how many different sizes of dog paws I could see and trying to guess what breed of dog they were. Eventually, we arrived at our second cairn with a wooden guide post directing the route we must take.

In springtime, Beetham Fell is draped in many delicate flowers, rockrose, harebells, wild thyme, and dropwort. Many years ago, the fell was open grassland, when it became devoid of continual grazing, it reverted to being colonised with many trees and shrubs providing a safe haven for wildlife.

As we were walking, we looked across at the large outcrops of limestone paving, reminding us of many wonderful walks we have done before in beautiful Crete. The gorges are littered with huge rocks and boulders of limestone; their deep crevices and fissures become home to shy geckos, snakes and adorned with delicate rock plants.

Leaving the leafy woodland behind us, we walked down a quiet country lane, climbing over another very narrow slip stile into a large field.

"Either my backside is getting bigger, or these old slip stiles are getting narrower," I complained, turning sideways and shuffling my way through.

Continuing with the walk, our map showed the way to a 'kissing gate' and onto the drive of Dallam Tower. A well-kept nineteenth-century house, part of which was built as early as the seventeenth century. Its angular and austere frame dominates the landscape overlooking a semi-circular driveway and is surrounded by immaculate lawns. The path leads us past the front of the splendid house and through another 'kissing gate' and into an immaculate deer park and grounds belonging to The Dallam Tower.

The views were lovely looking across towards the River Bela, which gently snakes through the large parkland. It was a good spot to eat our picnic and rest a while; we found a wooden bench conveniently placed near a line of newly planted trees. An old gentleman was in the process of feeding a few ducks by the old stone bridge along-side the riverbank. More ducks arrived, and the feeding frenzy increased and with it a cacophony of noisy quacking. Not to be outdone, a family of swans with their 'ugly ducklings' joined the increasingly large group. We noticed the signets, who had been born the previous summer, they still had a few pale brown feathers, but once these are gone, they would turn into beautiful swans like their parents. It's lovely seeing the little signets or ducklings riding along on their parents back, with others sheltering inside their large wings and resting for a while.

It was unwise to linger any longer than is necessary on such a cold day; the sweat on your body from walking starts to dry, and you begin to feel very cold. As soon as we had eaten our picnic and drunk the coffee, we set off again. Suitably replenished, we were heading towards the little market town of Milnthorpe over the bridge on the river Bela.

"We have had some lovely views of the snow-covered hills today," I said to Chris, as we walked into the busy town centre along with many afternoon shoppers.

Looking around Milnthorpe for a while and through the little shop windows situated in the square. A lovely variety of goods from homemade bread and pies to pretty gift shops, a master butcher who makes his own sausages along with some mouth-watering BBQ food. However, time was marching on, and we were only halfway through our walk, mindful of February's short days. Once the sun has lost its warmth, it will become increasingly colder and uncomfortable.

Re-tracing our steps, we walked alongside the River Bela once more, listening to the amusing sound of a few ducks making their familiar 'laughing' (quacking) sound.

"They're laughing at your woolly hat again, Patti!" Chris said, smirking at me and looking up at the hat perched on top of my head.

"Don't Care!" I retorted. "It keeps me ead wa-arm," I added in a broad Lancashire dialect.

Taking a quick detour to look at the lovely old Norman church and grounds nearby and read some of the oldest gravestones situated near the church door. When we are out and about in towns or villages, we try to do this as it tells you so much about the area and its people as well as being an important part of social history.

Leaving the town behind, we followed a path over another stile and into a frozen field. Walking down the field, we saw a lot of white billowing smoke coming from a tall chimney at the paper mill factory, outlined against the darkening sky. Carefully negotiating the busy A6 road, we crossed over to the other side of the road and onto a narrow path.

Hand in hand, I recalled the time when we had to cross the 12-lane main highway into the centre of Athens. We were staying on a caravan site with the motorhome for three days, and we had to get to the bus stop over to the other side of the road. We teetered on the edge of the curb, looking for a break in the busy morning traffic. Halfway across we realised we wouldn't make it across, even though we were walking quickly. Looking at the oncoming traffic, a young man was hurtling towards us in his fast-moving car. Instead of slowing down, he widened his eyes in horror and we turned and ran for our lives back to the pavement again. It took us a while to manage to cross all 12 lanes (six lanes going out of Athens and six lanes coming in with a central reserve). To top it all, when the bus finally came for us to get on it, we were not quick enough to get to the bus doors, the driver saw a break in the traffic, so he drove off again! It's not very often I am rendered speechless, but I was that day! Unbelievable!

Passing by the large paper mill buildings, we were crossing the River Bela again and walked back to our car in Beetham village. It was twilight now, and we decided to have an evening drink in the lovely Wheatsheaf Hotel and get warmed up by the fire. There is nothing nicer than lifting the door latch on an old oak-beamed country pub, where the heat from a cheery open fire hits you after being out in the cold all day and enjoying a good brisk walk. Our boots and gaiters were heavily caked in wet mud and we called out to the landlord to ask if it would be okay to come inside.

All the years we have been walking, we have never been refused entry to traditional country pubs, even when we have returned thoroughly wet through and the boots in a bad state. We have always been greeted with pleasant smiles and asked where we have been walking and what we have seen. Only once can we remember when we were politely asked to take our boots off and leave them by the door, which we did.

The traditional English public house serves as an important hub of the community, either meeting up with friends, having a meal together, playing darts or dominoes, where volunteer groups meet to organise events or a celebratory drink after scoring the winning points in the local football team. It's so sad that more and more English pubs are closing their doors for the last time, the advent of changing times due to drink/drive and no smoking inside the premises.

Today, a nice old oak-beamed pub is very much open for business, and we received our usual friendly welcome from the landlord. Quickly taking off our outer coats, hats and gloves, I found a cosy corner next to a roaring fire and leant my back against the old wooden settle, admiring the pictures, brasses, copper jugs and pewter drinking vessels.

Sipping my wine, Chris took a long drink of one of his favourite cask beers, which resulted in a frothy beer moustache!

It was my turn to take the 'rise' out of him!

"Let's have a game of dominoes," I said, reaching for a box of 'nines' (nine spots).

"I bet I beat you," I said laughing, and just under an hour later, I did!

"Three games to one Chris, ha ha…"

Chapter Two

'FEBRUARY FILL DYKE' – Living up to its name this year with the heavy grey skies producing continuous downpours of icy rain and sleet in the first weeks of February. Filling all the dykes, rivers and streams up to brimming. Walking is very difficult at times when your boots become so heavy with wet mud and muck from the farms and fields. Crossing fields and meadows, now totally sodden with many large puddles forming in the deep ruts and lower pastures. A feat in itself when you come to field gates, churned up with the feet of cattle and only a large stone or a piece of wood to step onto as you sink, ankle-deep into the mud.

Sometimes our boots and gaiters will submerge right up to your shins in the stagnant mud and water. I remember a time when we were out walking, and I thought there was an area just over the other side of a gate that looked solid; imagine my face when I jumped over the gate and landed square on into a deep slurry pit? I wasn't a happy bunny that day!

Each laboured step and careful negotiation through deep muck and water resulted in thick, cloying mud pulling at our boots, sometimes nearly pulling them off altogether as we cross over the fields and through farmyards to continue the walk.

"Why do we do it?" we ask ourselves when the heavy rain come to drench us through, but just around the corner or down the next lane, we see amazing views or remarkable things of interest. Then when the rain stops and the sun comes out, all is well again. We love to watch the changing seasons, the early snowdrop, crocus or daffodil. Beautiful Roe deer hidden amongst the trees in ancient woodland, their white bobtails quickly disappearing when they take to their heels and dash away from us. Dappled sunlight reflecting on undulating green hills and fells with swathes of purple heather snuggled amongst the tall ferns and bracken.

Listening to the sweet call of the birds high in the canopy of trees, a cheeky robin redbreast is hopping along the hedgerows in bleak wintertime, hoping for a treat. The quiet hush is broken by our walking boots as we trample on the autumn leaves in the dense woodland. I remember walking in Germany one day through a beautiful old woodland on our way to visit the chateau which was used in a Kronenburg advertisement for lager beer, it was early morning, and we were walking up the steep path through the woods, the sun was shining through the branches of the trees throwing bright shards of light onto the forest floor, now and again we heard the resonant plop of large conkers falling from massive chestnut trees above our heads. We stopped for a while and gazed up into the lush canopy of trees and breathed in the fresh morning air; it is times like this we feel at peace with the world and enjoy the ever-changing seasons.

There are the wonderful changing seasons of our beautiful England; with all its intemperate weather, we witness the unfolding beauty of nature and embrace all it has to offer.

We thought we would do a circular walk the next day, and we listened to the weather forecast that evening. The rucksack was packed again and ready to go with a medical kit, waterproof leggings, tissues/wipes, map and compass. All we had to do the next morning was make our usual picnic and fill the flask.

We usually walk 'off map' from the Ordnance Survey Map or pick a walk from one of our many walks books. When we have done it, I usually write a brief synopsis on how the walk turned out so we will know for next time.

The weatherman told us the day would be dry and settled here in the North West of England, with maybe some sunshine, a welcome change after all the cold weather this year. Although it hadn't rained for a few days, we knew that the ground would still be sodden. With this in mind, we took our gaiters along with us to wear over our walking boots and trousers, protecting our legs and covering the tops of our boots against deep muddy ruts and puddles.

We would be doing a six-mile walk today out of the Pendle Witches Trail book; having done one or two other walks from the same book, it is a very interesting area steeped in history and folk law. The area around Pendle Hill is surrounded by a few sleepy villages and hamlets; here, several ladies were accused and charged with the practice of witchcraft. It was in the year 1612 when Old Demdike and Chattox, two of the most well-known witches, were charged with this heinous crime. Tortured to get a confession, they were brought before Justice Roger Nowell, who sent them to Lancaster Castle to await trial. Old

Demdike died in prison before the trial through neglect and ill-treatment in prison. With unsanitary conditions and on a diet of bread and water, many died before having their sentence heard. On August 20, 1612, nine unfortunate women were convicted of witchcraft and hanged in front of a large crowd of jeering people. Their bodies were subsequently burnt and buried in un-consecrated ground. The only crime these old ladies did was to grow and use herbs for varying illnesses and treatments. Coupled with ignorance and fear from some other villagers or even dislike of their neighbour, they would report them to the magistrates without any proof needed.

Setting off from home early after breakfast, we drove for about an hour to reach the sleepy hamlet of Worston just off A59 in Lancashire and parking behind The Calfs Head Inn, claimed to be 250 years old. A low eerie mist hung over the fields as we approached the village, the air damp and still. Chris knocked on the back door of the Inn and asked permission to park the car there while we did the walk, with the promise to come back and have some refreshments. The landlord thanked him for taking the trouble to ask permission and said it was alright. The sun was breaking through the clouds as we pulled our walking boots and gaiters on, waterproof coats, hats and gloves.

Heading down the picturesque main street and passing several quaint cottages lining our route, our walks book tells us that the very small house to the left of the Hotel, a one up and one down cottage, once belonged to the convicted witch named Chattox. Getting into conversation with a local lady who was cleaning the cottage outside, she said she wasn't aware that the tiny dwelling once belonged to the notorious witch.

"I wonder if the cottage is haunted," I murmured to Chris as we started walking again.

Despite the cold, bracing wind, the day was just right for a good brisk walk, the watery winter sun climbing higher into the pale blue sky. The walk took us around the side of a house to a gate and stile into a field ahead. The views were lovely and dominated by the regal Pendle Hill in the distance, which we have already climbed before. Today would have been ideal because it was a bright clear day, with a 360-degree view over the distant hills and fells.

Ambling across two fields without much trouble, although still very wet in parts, we reached a small iron gate over a swollen stream and onto a sheltered track which meandered for a while through a sparsely populated area consisting of just two farms and two very old stately Halls, one of which is reputed to be haunted by an Abbot. The landscape changed dramatically near the top of the fells, no green buds on the ravaged windblown trees and the absence of wildflowers; instead, a bleak, cold and lonely place existed with only a hardy sheep farmer sitting astride his quad bike just a little higher up the fells from us. He was intent on bringing his ewes down to the lower pastures for the lambing season. Alongside him was his faithful sheepdog, who ran backwards and forwards to herd the ewes safely down the fells. We watched the clever sheepdog for a while before moving on again.

The track eventually led to the main road, and we crossed it to follow the signpost to the pretty village of Pendleton, to rest awhile and eat our picnic. Passing by the impressive All Saints Church on our left and the old village school built in 1837, we reached the centre of the village and sat down on a bench.

A narrow fast-flowing stream runs through the centre of the village, draining the fells above. Immaculate grass verges border either side of the stream, with many early daffodils coming into bloom in the afternoon sunshine. A row of little cottages was set back from the sleepy lane with pretty names as Christmas Cottage, Rose Cottage or Wayside. A mix of early spring flowers bordering their front stone paths, quintessentially English.

Tucking into our picnic, I turned my face up to the sun and closed my eyes for a while to listen to a mix of small birds twittering and singing in the trees and shrubs nearby. Presently, a couple of mature cyclists slowed down to look if the pub was open for business – it wasn't. They decided to continue their journey and shouted hello and waved.

Leaving the village of Pendleton behind, we climbed over another wooden stile situated in the corner of the field and followed a track that ran alongside a meandering stream and up to a large sloping field. We continued left for a while with Pendle Hill over to our right, along with a scattering of sheep grazing high on the fells where we had walked earlier. Heading back now, we passed the farmer we had seen earlier, still sitting astride his quad bike with his wife hanging on the back behind him and his sheepdog running alongside. He waved and shouted, "Do you know where you are going." Nodding furiously, Chris shouted back, "Yes, thanks."

He was systematically moving his herd of sheep further down into the lower fields with the help of his dog moving in the familiar zig-zag direction, constantly attentive for any ewes breaking away from the rest. Occasionally he looked at his master for instruction or even approval.

"No wonder that dog is all muscle and sinew; he's constantly on the go," I remarked as we started walking again.

"Sheepdogs love to work; he's doing what he knows and what is bred into him," Chris replied. "He's a happy dog; look at his tail constantly wagging."

Arriving back at The Calf's Head in the village, we walked to the car and removed our muddy boots and gaiters and replaced them with lighter shoes. Lifting the metal door latch, we stooped down under a low wooden beam over the doorway and onto the well-worn curve of the stone step.

We were temporarily blinded coming in from bright sunlight to the contrasting gloom of the pub's interior with all its dark oak beams and furnishings. A cheery blaze in the hearth welcomed us as we sat down and talked about the events of the day and our lovely walk.

Chapter Three
Pendle Hill

March

It's been a healthy outdoor tiring week; we have done three good walks on three different fells.

Recently, the weather has made marked improvements, no rain for two or three weeks but strong winds and watery sunshine helping to dry out sodden fields, fells and tracks and making it a lot easier to get about.

Mad March! This bizarre saying originates from the antics of boxing hares. We see them in the fields near our home by the Wyre Estuary in Lancashire. They are quite comical if you get a chance to see them yourselves. For many years I thought the participants were two males fighting each other for territory and female attention. However, this is not the case; it is a female hare fighting off her many suitors at the same time. When the strongest suitor wins, he will couple with her. The poor creatures must be exhausted!

In the pleasant early sunshine, the snowdrops are fading now, but the beginning of many yellow swathes of daffodils growing wild along roadsides. They border many towns and villages, growing wild in fields and under hedgerows. It is a welcome sight in England after such a long winter and heralds the start of springtime along with delicate primroses and celandines growing in tiny clusters in woods or rough pasture land.

We made arrangements with friends to do a walk up to the top of Pendle Hill. Rising 1,831 feet at its highest point, it dominates the pretty farming landscape below. Our walks book guide leads us straight up the centre of the Hill, walking along the top ridge with a graduating descent down the 'shoulder' of Pendle, completing a popular circular walk.

With light rain overnight and some in the early morning, we drove out towards the tiny village of Barley which nestles in the foothills of Pendle Hill.

The rain had stopped, and we were blessed with some watery sunshine breaking through the heavy rain clouds with the hope of a fine day.

"The weather at the top of Pendle can change so quickly," Chris remarked, "A sudden mist or low cloud drops without warning, making visibility poor and sometimes dangerous."

We were meeting our friends in the car park nearby; they had already arrived and waited patiently, changing into our walking boots with map and compass; we hoisted the rucksacks on our shoulders and set out on the walk.

The little village of Barley is steeped in ancient history with many mystical origins. Not only is it well known as the main area where the legendry Pendle Witches lived and met around Barley and Pendleton. In 1646 George Fox was said to have preached the gospel of love and founded the Quaker Movement. At the end of November 1536, there was a rebellion against the suppression of the Catholic religion by Henry V111. Although there was some loyalty to the King, there was also a great need for freedom of worship. Consequently, beacons were built on Pendle Hill, and their lighting was a signal and a summons to arms.

It is little wonder then with all the historical activity and pilgrimage over many years, resulting in smooth, well-worn paths, zigzagging up the Hill and along its 'shoulder' with many more leading off in different directions. Many people make a pilgrimage on All Hallows Eve, 31st October when witches and ghouls are meant to be abroad.

We chose to take the direct route up to the 'trig point', gaining height quickly and hopefully being able to admire the views towards the Forest of Bowland, Ribblesdale and Craven Fells, and in the distance, the Lakeland Fells. We were lucky that day to be able to gaze across at all the various landmarks shown on the top of the stone 'trig point'.

Having done this same walk to the top of Pendle in 2006, we stayed overnight in our motorhome on a caravan and camping site nearby. We remembered descending Pendle Hill with the threat of heavy summer rain along with a constant rumble of thunder some distance away. Some well-placed but slippery stone steps are leading from the 'shoulder' to help walkers down, but many others were coming up on the same route. The winding path is steep and narrow, and whilst we were coming down, many others were climbing up to the summit. We were surprised to see a young couple coming up towards us carrying a picnic basket. He had a pair of sturdy shoes on to tackle the slippery, uneven path, but the young lady had on a pair of plastic flip flops and kept slipping on the smooth, greasy stone steps.

I was concerned for her safety, and helpfully, I told her the terrain was a lot worse the higher you go; she could slip and hurt herself. Beaming back at me, she said, "Oh, I have already slipped twice, but he (pointing to her husband) wants to have a picnic up there." We were astonished and shook our heads as a light rain began to fall, and the thunder got louder, eventually breaking into a torrential downpour with a dramatic thunderstorm just as we got back to our motorhome.

Warm and dry, we sat watching the theatrical drama of the summer storm unfold through the windows of our van. I wondered if the young couple were alright and hoped they had got back down safely again.

Over many years of walking and sightseeing, we have seen some quite dangerous, remarkable or even hilarious sights on occasion. We have administered first aid to a few people both in England and abroad, on the hills and fells and in the mountains of Greece. I remember seeing a young lady and her boyfriend on the Bowland Fells one lovely summer's day. Both had sensible walking shoes on, but the young lady wore only a tiny bikini as they walked hand in hand in the sunshine through bracken and heather moorland.

Another time, we were coming back from a holiday in our motorhome from the Lake District, driving along twisting roads over the tops of remote moorland, when we saw a motorbike rider skid across the road in front of us and plunged down the embankment before crashing head-on into a dry stone wall. He went flying over his bike and laid very still on the grassy bank; we stopped to see if we could help. By then, his mates who had been riding with him had also stopped and come rushing over. The injured man was conscious, and I dropped to my knees to help him. He was fully kitted out in leather motorbike gear which, in my opinion, saved his life. His helmet was badly dented and scratched, and one of his mates gently removed the helmet when the poor lad began to hyperventilate with shock. As it was a very hot day, he grew increasingly uncomfortable, so when one of his friends called for an ambulance, I gently checked him over for broken limbs etc. and found one of his wrists had been broken.

He was wearing large leather gauntlet gloves, and he said he could feel his hand and wrist swelling inside. I asked him if he wanted to ease it off before the swelling got too big because the ambulance men would cut his glove off so the doctor could set his wrist. He agreed, and between us, we slowly and carefully eased the glove off a finger at a time, he was fully concentrating on this procedure, and his breathing was calming down.

The shock was setting in when he realised the enormity of what had happened. He was sweating profusely in his leathers. I asked him if he would like some water to make him comfortable until the ambulance arrived. One of his mates had phoned his mum and bent down to let him speak to her. That helped; it took his mind off how lucky he had been to just have a broken wrist.

Apparently, his bike had hit a patch of oil on the road and, losing control on the bend, skidded off and hit the stone wall. We think God must have been watching over him that day.

On holiday on the pretty island of Rhodes one year, we hired some pedal bikes to ride up into the hills for some sightseeing and a picnic. Cycling along for a while, we admired the magnificent views of the hills and mountains, eventually stopping at the side of the road by a small marble quarry to rest. Many local vehicles were rounding a sharp left-hand bend and passing us by, was a young man and woman on a 'twist and go' motorbike who came riding up the hill towards us. Suddenly the front wheel of his bike hit some rough loose stone and the bike shot from under him. He flew over the handlebars into the road at our feet, and the young lady fell to one side into a deep ditch, landing on her back. Judging by the amount of screaming she was doing, we thought she had broken her back. Chris went over to him; he had managed to get up again unaided, although his knuckles had all been ripped wide open, exposing some bone and pouring with blood.

As Chris tended to him with antiseptic and first aid dressing, I was on my knees comforting the young lady and administered first aid. Checking no bones were broken, I helped her sit up and gave her a sip of water. She had fallen heavily onto some large rocks within the ditch. A local man had stopped in his pickup truck and offered to drive them back down to the town with their bike. At first, the young man refused and said he wanted to carry on. Chris had a quiet word with him and said they would both be in shock and very bruised, and it was not advisable to get back on the bike.

He eventually agreed, and they got their lift back down the hill and to the village. We wondered how they had gone on when we returned to our hotel that evening. The shock and severe bruising don't always show up right away; we hoped it didn't spoil their holiday.

Back to My Story

Leaving the 'trig point 'and a few weekend walkers, we decided to find a sheltered spot out of the wind to eat our picnic. The sun had managed to peep through the heavy clouds; we could feel its warmth and found a place behind a dry-stone wall to sit down on our waterproof leggings and eat. Munching away in companionable silence, our attention was drawn to other people and their dogs walking by us. One particular dog, a black Labrador, spotted us from a few yards away and came bounding over towards our friend who was sitting next to me. Without slowing down or missing a step, the dog stretched his neck up to her hand, holding her sandwich and gobbled it up, then he bent down and stuck his nose in my coffee cup and slurped a few mouthfuls of coffee! But that wasn't all; he spun around again and snatched another sandwich out of Chris' hand on the return journey.

We all looked at each other in astonishment as the cheeky dog galloped back to his owners as if nothing had happened. They had seen their dog snatch the food, and the guy came over and apologised for his dog's bad behaviour. We all saw the funny side of it and laughed it off.

Today, the paths and hills are quite busy with small parties of youngsters and adults enjoying the good weather. It has its downside; however, you are unlikely to see any wildlife up there, only bracken and scrubland, but the views are lovely. Walking along the top of the ridge, the backbone, the views became limited when a low cloud descended, followed by a fine misty rain. With heads held low against the icy cold wind and squalling rain, we made a slow descent, with some of the uneven paths becoming slippery with the onset of wet weather. Further down the hill, the rain stopped as quickly as it had started, and we realised it wasn't rain but a very low cloud.

Back at the car, we changed out of our wet coats and boots and said a fond farewell to our friends who we would be meeting up with again in Crete very soon.

Dunsop Fell and Croasdale – Eight Miles

The settled weather continued, so we decided to do another walk from our Bowland Walk's Book. Leaving behind the weekend walkers and strollers, we started on a cloudy but dry morning with a sharp nip in the air to remind us we were still in the month of March.

A long slow climb of a one in three for approximately three miles up Dunsop Fell, stopping now and then to catch our breath and admire the views. Chris said, "He prefers to get the steep climb out of the way first, and the higher we went, the better the views at the top." We never feel the need to rush on a walk; why would we? We don't have to prove anything to ourselves or others; it's not a race after all. We walk for pleasure, a good day out in the fresh air, wildlife, scenery to end with a picnic, lovely!

A blanket of peace and tranquillity descended, the silence broken occasionally as skylarks call to each other high above our heads as we made the slow ascent to the top of Dunsop Fell. Climbing steadily along the rough pastures and sunken pathways, crossing a series of becks, fast-flowing and clear with constant drainage. Nearing the cairn, we pause to look at the spectacular views over to Easington Fell, the nub of Pendle Hill. In the distance, the smooth glassy surface of Stock's Reservoir, framed by the dense green Gisburn pine forest. Visibility was good, and we slowly moved around to get the excellent 360-degree views.

For a further ten minutes or so at a steady pace, we levelled off as we reached the top of the Fell. Walking onto the open moorland, bleak and ravaged due to continually harsh weather conditions. The strong icy March winds whipped at our clothes and stung our faces as we followed the direction in our walking book. Jumping and skirting around large boggy areas and marshy ground to avoid sinking in and always mindful of the danger it can present This is where the sensible experience of walking comes into its own, so quickly a situation can get out of hand. A brief moment in concentration and forward observance can see a novice walker step into a bog and get sucked down into the mire. It is advisable NEVER to walk on your own on the moors, carry a mobile phone and tell someone where you are going.

The walks book tells us to aim for a drystone wall directly in front of us and about one mile away. We could see a red flag waving about as a marker in the strong North winds in the distance, but we had to negotiate a lot of waterlogged marshland first. Picking our way through the difficult terrain, leading us away from the original path, the conditions deteriorated further. After some discussion, we decided to come back down the other side of the Clough, missing part of the walkout because it didn't seem safe or advisable to continue further.

We were now walking on level terrain once more and crossed a narrow stream that ran down from the fells to follow a narrow dirt track path leading to the back of Croasdale House. We followed the last remaining directions in the book and turned to follow another single-track road to eventually bring us back into the village of Slaidburn.

Leaving the rucksacks in the car, we walked over to the pretty roadside inn called The Hark to Bounty for a rest. Talking to the landlady later, we said we had to shorten the walk because of the dangerous conditions up there. She said an elderly man had gone up there on his own a few weeks ago and didn't return. The police were alerted, and a thorough search was made to look for him. Last week they found the man's body in a deep bog he had got into difficulties and drowned.

Parlick, Fair Snape Fell and Saddle Fell – Nine Miles

Early morning saw the day dry and bright with good visibility and plenty of sunshine, just right for a walk on the fells and hopefully some excellent views.

Boots, map and compass, gaiters, waterproof coats, hats and gloves to protect us against the strong March winds.

In a direct route up Parlick Pike, there would be an ancient cairn waiting for us, dating back to prehistoric times, along with a shelter for the avid walker for some protection against the harsh elements. We stopped for a rest now and again to catch our breath and gazed across towards the Fylde Coast and the South. Unfortunately, a low mist was descending to obscure further views.

We continued north along a fence line to the Col. F, following an obvious track to Fairsnape and another large cairn in the distance to mark our way. A few walkers were ahead of us, with some coming up behind, far enough away to give each other the space and privacy most walkers crave. It is strange; with so many walkers, it seems an unwritten rule not to pester or crowd each other but respect each other's privacy. At this point, we had been walking for a while and found a sheltered spot, possibly a sheep shelter, out of the strong winds to enjoy a welcome cup of hot coffee and a sandwich before moving on.

As we turned onto the continuing path, deep bogs and hags on each side became apparent. However, the path was well-trodden in parts we had to keep to the fence line and cross, intermittently over well-placed stiles in the fence to advance with our walk.

We were now coming to a large open space, where peat was still being extracted in large quantities behind a newly fenced area. Several large bags were already filled and waiting for someone to come and collect them in an all-terrain heavy vehicle. We had spotted some large tyre marks leading up to the gate and inside the perimeter. Moving along the line of fence, we were jumping over and skirting around the dangerous boggy areas and marshy ground to avoid sinking in over our knees. There was real danger here!

My sound advice from the last walk proved itself a few minutes later when we saw four men walking towards us on the opposite side of the boundary fence, which we had been following in our walks book. Greetings were exchanged, and we told them about the boggy areas further down and advised them to use the wooden stiles, which were placed across the boundary fence every few hundred yards or so.

One guy looked white-faced and shaken as he told us that just half an hour ago, he had stepped into what he thought was a hard surface, when in fact, it was a deep bog. He immediately sunk up to his knees and couldn't move. His mates had to pull hard on his upper body and eventually got him out again!

You could see he was still in shock and added, "If I had been on my own, I wouldn't have been able to get myself out at all."

As we continued, not long after the conversation with the four guys, the path ran out. We had been busy concentrating on skirting the many bogs and marshes; we had been grossly detracted from our route and lost our way! Out came Chris' compass, and he took an accurate reading, placing it on the map then pointing to the direction that we must take.

We were heading away from the peat bogs now, and I offered a silent prayer for our safety. Our feet and legs were very tired and aching as every step over soft marshy land sucks at your boots, and lifting your feet become extra weight. Then soft bog land disappeared and in its place were large swathes of heather not yet in flower, along with high knolls of grasses and bracken, which would eventually take us back to civilisation. Many wild grouse were disturbed by our slow, plodding footfall, flying up in front of us and making loud cackling protests at being disturbed from their well-hidden nests amongst the bracken.

Alone now! No other human being or animal were anywhere near us, no grazing sheep, no sound, not even the wild birds as we systematically moved across the bleak open moorland.

"We're not lost, are we?" I shouted above the strong wind, which whipped my words away and caught my breath, battering my face and clothing.

"No, we are Not Patti; stop worrying, just follow me. The compass never lies!" Chris shouted back a few feet in front of me and striding out.

"Come on, we will have a rest shortly around the side of this hill and out of the wind to eat the rest of our picnic," he added.

Ten minutes later, we found a deep grassy ridge with many wild and magnificent views across a deep cleft etched out with the constant rushing rain water coming down from the fells. A few sheep were grazing on the slopes, so far away they looked like children's toys. As I brought the picnic and flask out of the rucksack, Chris was looking at the map and walks book, and with the aid of his compass, he confirmed that we should reach a farm shortly just over the next ridge.

Munching slowly on my sandwich and in deep thought, I listened for any possible noise around me. I could hear the melodic sound of skylarks high above us feeding on the wing, but that was all. The sun was warm on my upturned face, and closing my eyes for a moment, I felt utter peace and contentment within.

With the sandwiches eaten, the flask drained of coffee, we packed up, making sure we hadn't left any rubbish behind. We set off again with renewed energy. It always seems difficult for me to walk on the side of a steep hill because my feet get misplaced inside the boots. A little while later, we began to descend towards the fast-rushing mountain stream we had seen earlier. Signs of civilisation became apparent in the form of a tumbled down sheep shelter, converted into pens for breeding grouse before letting them loose on the moorland. It's big business these days with many folks coming for a day's shooting.

We remembered doing a lovely walk along the top ridge of High Street, an important Roman Road and staying in a farmhouse accommodation in the village of Askham. We were walking on the tops, and a plump grouse bird was coming slowly towards us. In fun, I said in a loud voice, "Hello," and to our amazement, the grouse immediately answered back in a high pitched, distinctive voice – "Hello." We both started laughing and then repeated our 'hello' a few times, and each time the funny grouse replied and followed us for a while. Tired of the game, we ignored it and continued on our walk, but shortly afterwards, the grouse flew up onto Chris' shoulder and made himself comfortable until he shooed it off. We could only hazard a guess that the grouse had been bred and held in one of the grouse pens; maybe the farmer had spoken words of 'hello' when he came to feed the birds.

"I think we will walk back along the quiet lanes now, Patti," Chris said, studying his map, "I think we have had enough excitement for one day." It was a lovely end to the walk actually as we listened to the birds singing and turned along the permitted path and onto the private driveway of Wolfen Hall, set in immaculate grounds with a fast-flowing stream running alongside the path. We stood watching a hang glider flying over the fells for a while before continuing our walk.

Swathes of beautiful yellow daffodils had been planted by the gardener at the Hall some years ago, and all along the riverbank, they nodded their heads in the bright afternoon sunshine, an occasional gust of the sharp March winds sent them into a sudden frenzy.

Eventually, we reached the pretty village of Chipping and call at The Sun Inn for a rest, discussing all the excitement and adventure we had experienced. It's a family-run pub and very friendly; we got into conversation with a member of the family who asked us where we had been. We told her about the four guys we had met and mentioned the guy who had got into difficulty in the peat bog. Nodding sagely for a moment, she told us that they had heard many tragic stories similar to this over the few years they had run The Sun Inn, and great care must be taken at all times.

Chapter Four
Heathwaite Coastal Walk – Five Miles

April

A cold, blustery morning at the beginning of April made us decide to look for a flight out to Crete and stay until the end of July. We found one at a reasonable price, flying out on Friday,13th April. We have booked flights before on this date and always found them to be a bit cheaper – could it be that some people are superstitious? We think so.

With a brief spell of hot weather, we decided to do a walk and picked a pleasant coastal walk starting from the shops at Arnside village pier. The present pier was built to replace the one destroyed in the storm on the night of January 31, 1983. The replacement money was collected by public subscription, and the new pier was officially opened to the public on April 12, 1984, just over a year later!

Walking away from the pier along the promenade, we pass the stately Albion Hotel towards the road end. The path soon deteriorates beyond the coastguard station and out to the Kent Estuary. Following the tiny well-trodden path alongside the beach, skirting boulders and washed-up beach detritus, we realised we had made the mistake of wearing too many winter walking clothes. Heading towards the farm at New Barns and just before the buildings, we turned left along the track and passed by a large caravan site to our left.

Once past the caravan site, the path leads you up towards a delightful woodland overlooking the spectacular cliffs around 'Arnside Point'. Huge swathes of bright yellow daffodils nod their heads in the gentle winds blowing from the Estuary. We duck under a lush green overhang of deciduous trees to follow the narrow winding path along its length.

Stopping to read the warning of 'extra care should be taken above the cliffs, the tides and quicksand in the bay are extremely dangerous' brought back memories of the day we walked alongside the bogs and hags recently.

Finding a bench overlooking the estuary, we paused for a while to have a break, peeling off some of our heavy winter clothing as the hot midday sun beat down on us.

The path eventually rises and becomes a track, following it to its end; there are some large blocks of limestone laid across it, so we take the left-hand fork along the road and through another caravan site to the hamlet of Far Arnside. In the seventeenth century, more people were living in Far Arnside than in Arnside itself. We were heading towards Copridding Wood and New Barns Bay – another delightful walk through the beautiful old wood managed by The Woodland Trust. The trees are coming into bud, and the birds are singing their springtime songs. Our feet crunch on fallen tree branches whilst the sun makes dapple light and shade through the treetops. We are returning to Arnside village after doing the splendid circular walk, one we would recommend because it is an easy and picturesque walk.

The cold, blustery weather in England has returned with a vengeance, with snow in Scotland on the high ground. The weather forecast was for the snow to come down from Scotland and the North East of England; instead, it has been lovely with warm sunshine but a cold, bitter wind in shady areas. Our thoughts are turning to our holiday in Crete; we already know the weather will be better over there. As we have had another cold, wet winter in England, we are looking forward to the warm settled weather of Crete; then we can walk to our heart's content.

At last, it is the morning of our holiday, and we were up early to finish packing and getting organised before the taxi came at noon.

We were off!

Everything went well, and as we were sitting in our seats waiting for take-off there was a pungent smell of burning coming from the back of the plane. This was followed by a lot of dashing up and down the aisles by the stewards until the pilot finally announced 'due to a technical fault he had requested the airport engineers to come and check it out'. Another hour passed by with some more flustered activity before the pilot announced that 'although the fault has now been repaired, he would prefer to change planes, and head office will be sending a plane from Luton Airport'.

Loud moans and groans came from the passengers as the pilot taxied back to where we had boarded earlier. We had to wait for further instruction after disembarking and wait in the lounge area. Chris bought two gin and tonics, and we ate the rest of our picnic, which we had made up that morning. By now, it was almost 6:00 pm. the day had almost gone, and we were still at the airport.

"Oh! What a long day it's turning out to be," I said as we joined the queue to board the plane which had arrived from Luton Airport. Fortunately, the pilot made good time, and we arrived at Heraklion Airport just before 2:00 am. We collected the hire car from the airport and apologised to the guy for being so late. A few minutes later, we were on the National Road heading towards our villa. The roads were quiet, and as it was the Cretan Good Friday (not always the same week as our Easter, it is a moveable feast), the locals would be with their families, getting ready for the celebrations at the weekend.

Our villa was very dirty, of course, it was! We had been away since November 2011; I think that all the bugs from the olive groves had found their way under the front door seeking refuge from the heavy rains of January and February. We always pull the furniture into the middle of the room and cover everything with dust cloths.

There is still quite a lot of snow on the Psiloritis Mountain range, which are nearest to our villa, coupled with a lot more snow on the Lefka Ori (White Mountain) ice and snow are apparent up to June.

It was very quiet as we pulled up outside our villa early morning along with a lovely clear sky, we looked up to see a twinkling mass of bright stars. With the absence of pollution or street lights, you could see very clearly the nearest constellations. It is an astronomers dream here, sometimes we lay on the sunbeds in the evening by the pool and see shooting stars.

I made the bed up, it felt damp and cold but there wasn't any alternative – it was very late (or very early! depending on how you look at it) by then, and we hoped we would get a few hours' sleep. Quickly wiping the fridge/freezer out, we turned it on so we could shop later and fill it with food.

We woke the next morning to a dog barking in the distance along with the tinkling sound of sheep bells as they grazed in the olive grove behind the villa. Rousing myself, I looked at the clock and was astonished to find it was 10:45 am Greek time, there is a two-hour difference and our body clock was still set for 8:45 am. Leaping out of bed we got ready to go down to the village and buy our groceries.

Parking the car under the canopy, a little gypsy girl shyly approached us smiling and muttering something indecipherable, we knew she was after money. By the side of the supermarket door, her mother was sitting on the floor nursing a young baby in her arms. With her calloused hand held out, coupled with a pained and sorrowful look on her weather-beaten face, she begged for money whilst her baby lay sleeping. We are accustomed to seeing them here on a regular basis as they live in a traveller's camp nearby.

The remaining Easter Saturday was taken up cleaning the villa and airing all the rooms, bedding and clothes. There had been a leak throughout the winter, raining in on the flat roof. There were some stains on the units and a great deal of water staining inside the cupboards. Chris said he would phone the builders after the Easter holidays to come and take a look.

It was early evening by the time we had made the villa clean and comfortable again, so grateful to sit down on the settee with a welcome glass of local wine.

"Here's to the start of our holidays," Chris said grinning. "YAMAS"

"Yes, cheers! Happy holidays," I replied, laughing.

Chapter Five
Easter Sunday (Paskha) – Crete

On Easter Sunday afternoon we drove out of our village and onto the National Road, it would take us a good hour or so along the winding roads, passing through many mountain villages and hamlets, on our way to see our friends in Asomati School who own and run a small taverna in the village. In the ancient village, there is an abandoned Monastery with a current undertaking of remedial renovation work to restore it to a museum.

There was still quite a large amount of snow lodged in the deep clefts and ridges from the previous winter. The snow glistened and sparkled in the afternoon sunshine giving a blue-tinged effect, reflections from the sun.

As any walker will tell you, you cannot fail to appreciate the ever-changing seasons, being so close to nature with the migratory birds and stunning wildlife in Crete. There is one creature, in particular, we call a 'humming bee'. It hovers very fast over open flowers, and when you look closely, you can see its tiny proboscis dip gently into the flower head.

One year when we were at our villa during the summer our friend who bred canaries said we could look after one for the duration of our holiday. We were pleased as we love to listen to their beautiful song and fuss over them. One morning we went to collect our holiday canary, astonished when our friend took us to the back of his house and showed us a huge aviary of many different coloured canaries.

"I thought they were only yellow, but these are every colour you can think of," I said as he picked out a young bird which he said sung very well. I was a bit disappointed that my little bird was the buff colour of a sparrow, but once we got him home and settled him into his cosy corner of the room; he began singing his beautiful songs. We called him Super Mario!

Over the summer we had such good fun with him and bought him several things for his cage to make him feel at home, a plastic bird, a mirror, a bell. He would sometimes cuddle up to the plastic bird especially in the evening and chunter quietly until he went to sleep. With the mirror, he was fascinated and kept peering behind to see if he could see another bird. The louder we were with our radio or the hair dryer, the louder Mario would sing to try and outdo them. I was sad when it was time to go back to England and return him to our friend's aviary.

Arriving in the village we parked outside the taverna and we could see all the family sitting around a large table eating their Easter lunch. They recognised our car and Vasilis got up from the table and came outside to greet us and invite us in. The metal BBQ roaster outside was full of succulent lamb cooking on the spit. Papa Manolis was sitting outside with two of his friends and jumped up as we approached, grinning broadly he shook hands with Chris and kissed me on both cheeks as is their custom. I peeped around the taverna door and spotted their wives Tina and Konstantina.

"Yassas," I called loudly and started laughing, they looked puzzled for a moment before realising who we were.

This followed with lots of Oh's and Ah's – hugs and kisses and hearty back-slapping from one man to the other. I had brought them all a little present for Easter, handing them out we wished them 'Kalo Paskha' (Happy Easter). I had made a needlepoint picture for Konstantina and Tina, I had knitted a little hat and cardigan for the baby. She hugged me tight and tears ran down her cheeks, she was pleased with such a personal gift.

I looked across at Manolis, a man of a few words at the best of times, but on this occasion, he got up and gently touched the tiny lace garments with his huge farmer's hands and remarked how small they were.

We thought they may have been closed in the taverna, it being Easter Sunday and asked Tina if they would serve us their delicious food. She replied, "You will be eating with us, Vasili's two brothers will be coming to join us later and we want you to meet them." Konstantina brought us a carafe of her home-made red wine then set about dragging two tables together.

The traditional Paskha feast is BBQ roast lamb, very traditional at Eastertime and other festivals and family celebrations, they usually put a half or whole young lamb on a large BBQ spit outside. Today, the succulent lamb will be from Manolis sheep farm nearby. We watched Tina and her mother prepare large bowls of salad and herbs, locally made feta cheese along with freshly cooked thick chips! The tables were filling up with a delicious array of food and in the centre was the largest plate of succulent roasted lamb, brought in by Vasili. Konstantina balanced a basket of homemade bread on the edge of the table. The feast was ready! Konstantina's two handsome sons appeared, we heard later that one son is engaged to Tina's sister.

No one stands on ceremony at a Cretan feast, I saw Manolis keep nudging Chris, encouraging him to dig in, whilst Konstantina kept pointing to different plates for me to do the same. Eating is a very important social affair and the Greek people love to dine out with their large families at any giving opportunity.

Looking up from my delicious plate of food I saw everyone laughing and talking as they ate and thought how nice this little Greek family was and how loving and close-knit they all are. I caught Konstantina's eye and she grinned back at me with her greasy mouth, chin and fingers! I just love all this! And looking over to Chris, his face a picture, told me he was too.

I was almost fit to bursting by the time I finished my meal, although Konstantina gesticulated for me to eat some more. I held my stomach and groaned, this made her throw her head back and laugh. Through Tina translating, Manolis said that this was his second 'big meal' today, he had already eaten a large meal with friends outside on the terrace to celebrate Paskha. He added, there will probably be another one or two meals to get through with friends before the end of the day.

With the tables cleared away, Vasilis put some lively Greek music on and his brothers got up to dance. All the children are taught the traditional Cretan dancing and singing from an early age in schools. It was so nice to see the young men dipping and stepping in time to the music. Vasilis joined his two handsome brothers, what a lovely trio they made, jumping to the side and clicking their heels as the family clapped and cheered them on. The rowdy noise soon brought other local men to the taverna and with all the laughing and singing going on it was like a talent show.

An elderly man had come in and sat in the corner of the little room, he began clicking his nails to a beat, then closing his eyes he tilted his head back and started singing a lovely Greek ballad. The taverna fell to a quiet hush as we listened to his lovely song, this was followed by an appreciative round of applause. It seemed customary for everyone to do a bit of entertaining and Chris and me were encouraged to get up and do something.

As we were in the party mood now due to Konstantina's homemade wine and raki, Chris and I got up and did a rendition of 'My Grandfather's Clock' and 'The Grand Old Duke of York'. I don't think there was anyone there who knew what we were singing, but we got a lot of loud clapping and cheering when we had finished. Then we saw Vasilis standing behind the counter and realised he'd videoed it all. The rest of the afternoon was taken up with periods of Greek music the kind we could all get up and dance to in a circle, lots of laughing, joking and singing went on until early evening until we were all too exhausted to do anything more.

It was such a lovely Paskha celebration, but as the evening was fast approaching it was time to say goodbye and go down from the mountains again. With lots of hugs and kisses we wished them a Happy Easter with the promise of coming again soon.

The fiery sun was sinking slowly in the West behind the mountains, replaced with vivid red, blue and purple streaks painted across a pale blue evening sky. Passing by the spectacular Potamus Dam, constructed a few years ago to hold mountain water for the villages here about. Unfortunately, they had to flood one village in the process, when the water is low in the summer you can still see parts of the derelict walls and houses.

As we approached the ancient village of Agia Triada and home, we saw our friend Maria walking towards us so Chris stopped the car. Maria and George have a small farm at the side of the narrow road leading up to our villa. We have made friends with them over time and value their friendship. They have hens and two cockerels, a little dog, cats, rabbits, sheep and a nanny goat with two kids. Chris wound the wind down and Maria put her head through and asked us in for coffee. We sat down on her large comfortable settee whilst she disappeared into the kitchen for a while, she returned with a large tray holding Greek coffee and a large plate of homemade Easter biscuits. I groaned inwardly and glanced across at Chris who acknowledged my look of 'Oh! No! more food'. The Greek people always eat something with a drink, no matter what time of day, and to refuse their kind hospitality is unthinkable and rude. Maria said she had made the Easter biscuits that morning from a traditional recipe only made for Paskha. They were cut into a lovely design with a slight vanilla taste, quite hard in texture but delicious. George came in soon after from feeding his sheep further down the village and went for a shower, returning later and joined us for coffee and biscuits. I watched him break a biscuit into two or three pieces and drop them in his coffee, then scoop them out with a spoon and eat them. *Ah! That's how you do it,* I thought I would break a filling on the hard biscuits. We stayed chatting to them for an hour and George told us that his home was about 400 years old, he showed us three very narrow windows right at the top of the house near the roof. He said they were 'look out' windows rather like the long narrow ones you see in medieval castles in England, they are to watch for the enemy approaching from the sea. He laughed and said, "He thought they were used to fire guns at the enemy." *Which enemy,* I thought, *there has been so many countries who have invaded Crete over the centuries.*

We said our goodbyes with the promise to have a meal out with them in the next few days. It had turned out to be a really lovely day with lots of fun and laughter and a few unexpected twists and turns too!

The second week of April, 2012 brought strong southern winds blowing continuously across the island from the distant lands of the Sahara Desert via Libya. The local people here call it 'Gaddafi's Breath' because it blows so hard and covers everything in a thick yellow/orange coloured sand. Carried along on the winds come many large green loci who munch everything in the plant world, attacking our roses with gusto until there is just the stalk left.

Fortunately, that afternoon the sun was out even though it was blowing hard. I took advantage of doing some washing, putting a brick underneath the clothes maiden so it wouldn't take off.

The strong winds blew all that day and into the night, howling constantly around the villa and making a dreadful eerie noise down the chimney in the lounge. In the early hours of the morning, I was woken suddenly by a constant banging noise and went to investigate, it was some of the shutters which had come loose and swinging wildly in the wind. I opened the inner window and a gust of warm air rushed into my face; I was wide awake then. Padding back to bed I looked at Chris still in the land of nod and snoring gently, oblivious to it all.

I laid awake for the next two hours listening to the gradual build-up of the strong winds turn into a hurricane force, rattling the shutters and doors, whistling and whining down the toilet pan and the chimney-making such a din I was quaking under the duvet. Getting out of bed again, unable to settle, I decided to read in the lounge for a while until it subsided. The lights in the villa constantly flicked on and off as I tried to read to no avail. All the mains electric cables are strung overhead on poles, so any strong winds or bad weather they get disturbed, resulting in power cuts.

The next morning, the wind had subsided somewhat and it was a nice sunny day. There had been a power cut during the night after I had gone back to bed and it was still off when we got up so we drove into Rethymnon and had our breakfast in one of the cafés in the centre of town.

With a brief respite in the weather, we drove down to Mili Gorge to see our old friend who has lived in a cave for almost 30 years. We hadn't seen him since the previous year and thought we could all go out together for the day. It was so nice to see him and have a quick catch-up on our news and sit outside the cave entrance in the warm sunshine. He said he had done a walk over the top of Prasses Gorge with an old friend who is a keen ornithologist, and hopefully see some nesting Golden Eagles over on the opposite side of the gorge walls. We didn't need to ask twice and drove a short distance to Prasses village to start the walk, we knew the terrain would be difficult with the usual loose boulders and rocks as well as the familiar thorny shrubs which tear into your legs.

Following our friend along a series of narrow goat tracks, he pointed over to 'The Pulpit' – a large stone obelisk protruding upwards, a good seven-feet high and balanced on the edge of the top of the gorge walls. The sun had climbed higher in the sky with settled weather and a vivid blue sky as we reached our destination, we squatted down on some fallen rocks to take a welcome drink of water. Chris pointed to a flat piece of ground at the very edge of the gorge, and we tentatively peered down to the gorge bottom as the deep spring floods rushed fiercely over many large rocks and swirled around wild trees and dead shrubbery.

"Wow, it's so far down," I exclaimed, grabbing Chris' hand to steady myself. We've walked the Prasses gorge before but we hadn't seen it from way up here.

Suddenly, and without prior warning, we saw the most memorable sight – one, we shall never forget. A large Golden Eagle flew across the gorge towards us, checking us out! We were eye-level with him and could distinctly see his large hooked beak and amber coloured eyes. He flew gracefully round in circles for a while, riding the warm thermals rising up from the gorge below. A few moments later, the female joined him along with the young fledgling, then both adults flew underneath the youngster to encourage and help exercise its wings.

We were rendered speechless and stared, open-mouthed, at the incredible sight before us. Both adults were flying quite near us now, so near you could almost reach out and touch them, we could hear the whooshing powerful wings, marvel at their powerful beaks and piercing amber eyes, but the most wonderful thing of all was the bright morning sunlight shining down on the vivid golden colour on the top of their heads and their huge wings. We remarked about never seeing birds of prey from above before as we were doing, if you were lucky, you would sometimes see circling birds of prey from below, but most of the time they would be so high up you couldn't see their colouring. As if that wasn't enough of a treat, a few minutes later the adults and fledgling were joined by four other adult eagles making seven in all. We couldn't believe our luck and our friend said: "He'd booked them the night before to give us a good performance."

On the way back home we talked non-stop about the eagles and said we were going to find out as much information as we could about the Golden Eagles, this is what we found:

Golden Eagle, Aquila Chrysaetos. 75–88 cm. Adults varying shades of brown with golden feathers on the head. Immatures have a white tail terminating in a black band with lighter patches on the wings. Usually seen soaring above mountain slopes, though may hunt near the ground. May also be found at coasts and in woods and fields. Nests in trees or rock ledges. Flight is powerful, gliding or soaring with occasional leisurely wing beats. One to three eggs, scarcity in food may result in the strongest fledgling eating the others to survive. Incubation around February stays with the parents until full-fledged. Protected species in parts of England and Scotland with the R.S.P.C.A wardens.

Chapter Six
Mixorrouma Village – SIX KMS

May

We had planned to do a walk from the village of Mixorrouma which is situated near the large town of Spili. We were up and out before the sun got too hot, ready to do an easy circular walk in the mountains.

Parking in the quiet sleepy village of Mixorrouma, which nestles in the foothills of a series of large craggy cliffs and hillside to gradually descend into a pretty green and verdant valley below, sheltered from extreme weather conditions, where local farmers grow their vegetable and fruit crops.

Walking out of the village we followed the directions along a narrow road towards the hamlet of Frati as the road opens out onto some beautiful lush green countryside on our right and in the distance. A pleasant cooling breeze blew across the open valley as we walked at a steady pace in the gathering heat of the day. In the early springtime, colourful swathes of wild flowers and herbs grow in the fields and by the roadside. Large clusters of blood-red poppies nod their heads to greet us in the warm breeze as we passed by. Vivid yellow button-sized daisies grow in clusters along with the pristine white heads of wild chamomile with their delicate fern shaped leaves. Bright yellow broom grows in abundance, their sharp thorns protruding from thick branches; giving shelter to many colourful migratory birds and wildlife. The tall thick stalks of wild fennel, sometimes five or six-feet high like miniature trees, sway gently in the breeze, their springtime colour of yellow catching the strong sunlight. A strong heady perfume of all the lovely wild flowers and herbs fill the morning air and give us pleasure as we walk by. A sharp bend in the road and the loveliest views stretch out before us, just when we think we have seen everything at its best, we turn another corner to be wowed by some more fantastic views.

Walking onto a small piece of waste ground by the side of the road, we gaze down at a small and very beautiful gorge, the walls rising up in a series of craggy slate blue and grey peaks; their giant fingers point up towards the azure blue sky. Far below, a tiny dirt track snakes in and out between lush pasture lands with a small flock of sheep grazing contentedly. Tinny bells clanged around their necks as they move to reach another juicy morsel of grass and wild herbs. Total peace and tranquillity descended on us except for the occasional mewling from two circling buzzards, they were so high they looked like moving dots against the blueness of the sky. We stood motionless for a while taking everything in around us. The little road ran parallel to the gorge as we continued our walk. Our eyes were constantly travelling along its length where small pieces of land were partitioned off for the local farmers to grow their olives or grape vines in the shelter of the gorge. Planted in neat, straight rows giving maximum protection throughout the year, they will yield a rich crop to make olive oil and delicious local wine.

Over to the far side of the gorge, wild olive trees and shrubs grow in profusion, leading up to where the craggy gorge mouth narrows and becomes impassable. Birds sang in the sunshine and bees landed on the beautiful wild flowers as we entered the hamlet of Frati. Most of the houses had shutters across the windows giving coolness inside the homes. At the far end of the village stood a pretty church with a war memorial dominating the square, familiar in most towns and villages. We were now looking for the path to descend towards the head of the gorge, hoping this would provide some welcome shelter from the burning sun.

We have done many walks in Crete over the years and have experienced one or two mishaps and confusion when a wayfarer marker has disappeared, leaving us unsure of how to continue. It seems the Greek people as a whole do not pursue the pleasure of walking and sometimes cannot understand why tourists would wish to do so. Although the Cretan tourist board are beginning to understand the value of promoting marked wayfarer paths to safely help walkers from abroad to enjoy the Island.

As we reached the bottom of the gorge and onto the track leading away from the gorge mouth, several narrow dirt track paths run through the olive groves making it confusing as to which path we should take. With some effort and re-tracing our steps now and again we came upon a wide concrete bridge with the fast-flowing Kissamos River gushing and tumbling over many large rocks. Worn smooth with age, the crystalline melt water from the mountains ended with a sparkling waterfall over at the far end, surrounded by scrubby trees and shrubs jostling for light and space, thick vines and gnarled branches twine around each other in an attempt to reach a chink of light.

Tree roots resembling elephants' trunks are exposed above ground at the edge of the riverbank, the rich top soil had been systematically washed away in the harsh winter floods. The large snaking root tips curl into the river, we looked down amongst the roots to see many beautiful tiny coloured stones trapped under the impressive root system.

Sitting on a large boulder in the shade of an old fig tree we rested awhile and sipped our cool bottled water and listened to the steady tinkling sounds of the waterfall. We watched two or three beautiful dragonflies hover over the fast-flowing river, their delicate wings caught the sunlight in a shimmering turquoise blue as they darted around to catch a tasty morsel. It was quite a magical place in this green dell by the riverbank, and as I daydreamed in the heat of the afternoon, I thought that this could be a special place where elves and fairies lived. We could have stayed there forever, it was so tranquil, but we needed to press on.

Our walks book tells us we go over the bridge and climb up the steep track towards the little church situated further down the gorge. With backs bent and our heads down against the heat of the day, we climbed up the steep incline. Sweat was running down my back soaking my t-shirt, and pouring down my face into my eyes so I could hardly see, eventually, we reached the top of the dirt track road. The constant exertion and extreme heat had made me feel sick and dizzy so we found what shade there was near a clump of scrubby thorn trees. I bent forward panting, letting the blood run into my head so I would not faint. Chris saw how uncomfortable I was and said we must turn back once I had rested as it would be foolish to carry on in this heat. It was very tempting to carry on down the little pathway leading off to the left once the dizziness left me and I returned to normal, but Chris insisted we should go back the way we came and added 'we can always do this walk another time when it is cooler'.

I was very disappointed as we don't like cutting a walk short but safety comes first and I soon came to terms with the situation. Slowly, slowly (sega, sega) and with care, we took our time returning to the peaceful village of Mixorrouma and found a cool shady refuge in a very old traditional taverna on the main street to sit and relax and hydrate our bodies again. An hour passed by and we both felt rested and recovered, it was mid-afternoon by then and somewhat cooler. Chris asked the taverna owner where the ruined village of Ano Mixorrouma was, he pointed to an old wooden signpost, bleached almost white with age.

The old village was set a little way back from the exit point of Mixorrouma, as we walked around, we noticed that some of the villas were in the process of being restored, with a few others being occupied again. One or two had already fallen into such a bad state of dereliction, their roofs and walls caved in and broken away from the main structures. They were lying in large crumbling heaps inside the properties and small trees were growing quite vigorously amongst the detritus of where once would have been domestic bliss.

We peered inside one of the crumbling ruins to look at a recently completed roof restoration. New wooden beams were now in place along with some tiny residents! A beautiful and well-constructed swallow's nest hung in between the roof shafts. It was nesting time! And the proud parents constantly flew in and out with food for their little family. As the adult birds approached the nest, four tiny heads popped out, chirping loudly in competition with each other for their parents to feed them. We stood watching them for a while as they fed their little brood of chicks, both adults ignored our presence, flying low over our heads to continue feeding. Tip toeing away so as not to disturb them all, we wandered further down the broken cobbled avenue to another derelict house and looked at the remains of what would have been an impressively large stone fireplace offset in the corner of the main living area. In the walls crumbling remains next to the fireplace, there were some wooden slats still in place and a purpose cut stone recess where the lady of the villa would have stored her dry goods of salt and flour in large stone storage jars. Pausing again and looking around us, we could imagine how the little family living here a long time ago would have gone about their daily lives. Who were they? What work would her husband have done? How many children did they have? And why was the old village left abandoned and neglected? As the local people began to build again in the current Mixorrouma just a short distance away. We have heard many terrible stories during our time in Crete, with villages being 'sacked and burnt 'by various invaders, attacking the island through the centuries. Maybe it could be that when the people grew old and died, their homes were sub-standard and abandoned with the next generation re-building a new village nearby? We think it was probably a bit of both!

Chapter Seven
Crete, Greece

The weather continues to improve daily, much more settled now, a lovely fresh breeze early morning with hot sunshine towards lunchtime until six o-clock when it begins to cool off again. It is very pleasant to be able to potter around outside and tend to our colourful Mediterranean plants and shrubs until darkness falls. As I write in the evening, we are listening to some relaxing music with the patio doors open onto the garden. There is a peaceful silence, save from the occasional bleating from our friend's goats in a field nearby.

The next day we thought we would drive to the pretty village of Spili and do a walk we had seen in one of our books. Arriving after lunch, we noticed a new folk museum had just been opened that year and decided to take a look. Inside a very large barn were many ancient Greek farming tools and household equipment. Each room had been furnished to replicate the inside of a traditional villa. The living room held a large wooden loom, set up with horizontal threads and an unfinished garment of cloth attached. As we walked around the rooms it surprised us how many things were similar to what our grandparents and parents had used in their homes. We got into conversation with a nice young man who was studying archaeology at Rethymnon University, working there as part of his course work. He was very knowledgeable about most of the farming tools, crafts and kitchen implements, and asked us what the English names of them were. It passed a very interesting hour or so, comparing our Greek/English knowledge of the collection of antique equipment.

Leaving the coolness of the museum, the sudden heat and bright sunshine hit us like a wall. Blinded for a moment we decided to go and see our lovely friend, another George who has a taverna in the centre of Spili village. Greeting us like one of his family, George welcomed us in to sit at a table inside, out of the searing heat of the day. While he prepared our drinks and meze, our eyes travelled around the room admiring old photographs and memorabilia. A lovely picture of his wife was hung on the wall, smiling down at us, along with several other members of his family. Over in the far corner was his industrial sewing machine which he used in earlier days when he was a tailor. One or two other old Cretan men were sitting together at the next table, talking and enjoying their drink and meze (tasty morsels of meat/olives/tomatoes). Presently, George came with his tray and sat down nearby to talk to us. After catch-up with all our news, he disappeared behind his counter and came back a few minutes later with several shot glasses and a carafe of raki! *Oh, no!* I thought to myself, *here we go again.* We watched George go to each table and put a shot glass down for each customer and an extra one for himself. Over the next hour or so, George made his way to each table in turn and chatted for a while before pouring another raki into the shot glass.

"It's a wonder he can stand upright," I murmured to Chris and watching George knock back another raki in one gulp.

"He's is obviously use to it, and you must admit the Spili raki here is the best we have ever tasted, but we must make our excuses and go before we get as legless as George."

We said our goodbyes to George with the promise to come and see him again soon and decided to do a circular walk around the village.

Spili Village

Spili is a picturesque village located at an altitude of 430 metres and 28 kilometres southeast of Rethymnon town. Due to its fabulous location, the village offers an astonishing view of the sea, and the entire surrounding is filled with trees, fountains, springs, chapels and churches with many wonderful murals.

The main square of the village is lovely and has a fine stone fountain constituted by a row of twenty-five stone carved lion heads from where crystal-clear water flows. Spili means cave in the Greek language and it is not hard to see why when you stand in the village centre, then your eyes travel up towards the towering rock formations, almost surrounding the village with one or two natural rock caves. There are many caves on the Island, some natural and some purposefully cut by man and dating to when the Minoans lived there. Over the years they have been used for storage, hideouts and living accommodation, the caves at Matala were purposefully cut by the Minoans and occupied in the 1960s by hippies with some well-known rock singers such as Janis Joplin, Bob Dylan and Donovan.

The village is famous for producing unique weaving. The important battle of Mesara, one of the many against the Turkish occupation, took place in 1833 in the village of Spili and in 1941 the village was destroyed by the Germans during WW11.

Many pretty tavernas line the main street, along with some old local ladies selling embroidered cloths and crocheting in their tiny shops. There are some interesting Byzantine churches and a medieval tower for the ardent tourist to visit. It was late afternoon, and the restaurateurs were busily getting their outdoor BBQ's ready to cook their delicious roasted goat. We watched one guy threading large pieces of goat meat onto the large skewers in readiness for early diners.

Rethymnon Town and Old Town

The next day we had to go into Rethymnon to see Mr Manolis who designed and built our villa, to see if he could come and fix the leak in the apothiki (boiler room). As it coincided with my birthday, we thought we would go into the Old Town and look for a suitable place to have dinner later that day.

Once business was out of the way, we headed towards the beautiful Old Town of Rethymnon, steeped in history, with many countries invading the town over centuries. Narrow streets and high walled buildings were purposefully built for maximum coolness and shade and the haphazard 'rabbit warren' of alleyways confuse visitors. With consequence, we never get tired of wandering around the Old Town looking at the quaint, unusual shops, cosy tavernas and restaurants.

The beautiful Kara Pasha Mosque reflects the time when the Turkish invaders were here for over two hundred years. Just around the corner is one of several Turkish fountains. An elevated and ruined Venetian fortress dominates the landscape, built in the sixteenth century as a stronghold, it has a good vantage point for the sea and town. At the entrance to the Fortezza is the impressive archaeological museum displaying local artefacts from the Neolithic period in Venetian times which include bronzes, jewellery, sculptures and sarcophagi.

The impressive Venetian Rimondi fountain dating from the early seventeenth century, lavishly decorated with columns and lion's heads spewing cold drinking water, is popular with locals and visitors. Many tourists gather there to take photographs or have a drink in one of the lovely restaurants nearby. There is also a striking minaret in the Old Town, its name is Nerandzes Mosque, and if you are feeling energetic you can climb up its steep spiral stairways for fantastic views of the town. If you are feeling tired and in need of a rest, you could always walk into the beautiful central public gardens and sit in the parkland café for a coffee or fresh orange juice and a tasty snack. There you can listen to the migratory birds and watch the world go by and rest for a while until it's time to move on again.

We strolled around for a while, enjoying the busy, happy atmosphere and found a pretty taverna nestling in the Old Town. The taverna was owned by an Italian guy, smartly dressed in a black and white uniform, he greeted us by the large wooden doors, we stepped inside the lovely old courtyard enclosed in partially ruined walls, with a mass of red bougainvillaea cascading down its sandstone walls. Soft Italian music played in the background as we were shown to our table in a quiet corner. We ordered our drinks and took in the surroundings, admiring a delightfully ornate fountain that gushed spring water from several cherubs' mouths, they were surrounded by some grinning dolphins. The stone courtyard was dotted with clusters of lush green foliage and colourful exotic plants and flowers. The overhang of thick branches from the ancient walnut tree sheltered us from the direct heat of the sun, although bright shards of light still found their way into the courtyard, giving us a warm relaxed feeling.

"Cheers Patti, Happy Birthday!" Chris said smiling at me and chinking my wine glass. I responded and held the wine glass to my lips to savour the long cool drink of deliciously chilled local wine. We spent the remaining afternoon enjoying the beautifully presented Italian food in exquisite surroundings, laughing and talking, planning and dreaming about the forthcoming weeks here on our long summer holiday.

Returning home early evening, we sat outside to watch the remains of the beautiful sunset, sinking slowly in the West over the little gorge alongside our villa. The sunsets here are magnificent, colourful swathes of red, blue, yellow and gold light up the evening sky before darkness descends to be replaced by a black velvet sky with millions of bright twinkling stars. When it's too hot to sleep we lay down on our sunbeds and watch the night sky, and if we are lucky enough, we sometimes see shooting stars which are truly wonderful.

I always feel spiritual when I am out in Crete, whether it is because we are both more relaxed, coupled with the constant warm settled weather and being constantly out in the clean fresh air I don't know but it's fantastic all the same.

Our home is a short drive from the lovely beach of Platanas, a busy little town at its centre leading down the main street for some distance with many restaurants, tourist shops and tavernas along its length, this runs parallel to the promenade with a clean beach. We often drive up one of the narrow roads and stop just short of a boardwalk, then walk along the fine yellow sandy beach for a couple of hours. In the summer we take our sandals off and walk in the warm shallows, and in the winter, we beachcomb and look for driftwood for our fire. The salty wood makes for a hearty fire after we have dried it out for a little while, the best kind of wood to burn is dried olive wood, but even better is the olive wood roots; which burns very hot and slow. Most evenings in the wintertime we have a good roaring fire up the chimney back and put potatoes and chestnuts in the coal embers. The result is amazing but you get black teeth and hands with the potatoes, but it's worth it!

One sunny afternoon a few years ago we decided to go beachcombing, not for driftwood particularly, but just to see what the strong tides had washed up on the beach and do a walk. Chris doesn't do yoga but I do, and I closed my eyes, extended my arms – palms up to embrace the sound of the surging tide, feeling the warmth of the sun and light winds on my upturned face. Chris usually makes himself scarce and walks some distance away. On this particular day, I did just that, there wasn't anyone about at all – the beach was deserted so it was the right time. I had been meditating for a few minutes when I heard a regular drumming sound that caught my attention. "Ignore it," I told myself, but the drumming sound got louder and then stopped. I opened one eye and squinted up to see a young man sitting on his horse and staring down at me with a puzzled look on his face. Closing my eyes again I called out PASS and waved my hand at him to continue again. He did!

Chapter Eight
Voting Day in Crete

We made arrangements to go out for lunch one Sunday to the taverna in the Village of Asomati School, high in the Psiloritis Mountains. It has become a pleasant Sunday treat for us with the lovely family who owns the taverna and welcome us like one of their family.

A very pleasant drive through the picturesque mountains and around the head of the huge and recently built Potamus Dam, we drove down the sloping track road to see Asomati village nestling at the very bottom; sheltered on all sides by the grey craggy mountains rising up in the distance. It has always amused me in the winter to see a few tall palm trees and in the background a thick covering of snow on the mountain tops which usually stays until late June.

We parked the car under the shade of some large plane trees near the gates of the Asomati School Monastery. Founded in the second Byzantine period and referred in a local document in the thirteenth century as The Monastery of the Archangel Michael, an agricultural college has operated here since 1930. Today, the Monastery is being renovated and has an agricultural research department. Originally built as a Monastery and surrounded by thick massive walls it made a suitable fortress against some local rebels in the region. One band of rebels was the Chortatzis family, where today you can see a Chortatzis grave in a Byzantine church nearby. The Monastery was attacked and destroyed several times in 1812 by Turkish invaders. However, in the temple interior, you can still see icons of the Trinity dated 1619.

We were immediately spotted by the family and after much handshaking and kissing, we were invited to come and sit down near the bar area as a smiling Konstantina brought us a jug of her delicious homemade red wine and asked us to follow her into the kitchen to see what she had made that morning for today's lunch. Several large pan lids were lifted on the stove with clouds of steam rising up to the ceiling I chose the chunky stewed chicken, haricot beans in olive oil and tomato sauce with herbs, sharing a plate with Chris, her homemade stuffed vine leaves with a slight after taste of lemon. Chris had his favourite lunch of barbequed lamb, salad and chips which Vasili prepared on the outdoor BBQ on the terrace. He told us his father has two or three hundred sheep on his farm nearby for their milk, and when the milk dries up, they are killed for their meat and used in the taverna.

It was a veritable feast and we ate heartily as first one member of the family would sit and talk to us to be replaced shortly afterwards by another, cooking and serving other diners who came and went throughout the afternoon. I had almost managed to clear my plate and picked at the remains of the food, eventually giving in and leaning back on my chair gave a loud sigh and patted my stomach much to the amusement of Manolis who grinned back at me and laughed.

With the lunchtime rush over, Vasilis and Tina, came out of the kitchen to sit with us and talk. Vasilis told us it was 'Voting Day' and they would be putting their cross on the paper soon. Because the mountain villages are so remote and so far away from the towns, it is customary for the local politician to come to them so that they can place their vote. As we talked about our families, politics and the economy in both England and Greece we heard a car pull up outside the taverna. Vasilis jumped to his feet and smiling he said the local politician was here to take their votes.

"Come and meet him," he said to us, we followed him out onto the terrace where an elderly guy with thick white hair and a long straggly beard stood waiting patiently. He was quite tall and very thin, his shabby clothes hanging on him and draping around his stooping shoulders. His bird-like face with an extra-long pointed nose turned to face us as we approached, his pale blue rheumy eyes darted around as he quizzically stared back at us. We stood back as Vasilis spoke to him in rapid Greek, we think he must have introduced us to him because his serious face immediately turned into a thousand creases and his eyes became half-moons as they almost disappeared into a genuine warm smile of greeting. Smiling back and saying hello, we turned away from the voting table and disappeared back into the coolness of the taverna once again to see Tina still sitting at the table on her own.

"Are you going to vote?" I asked her as I took my place at the table with Chris.

"No, I'm not, I never do," came the solemn reply. We told her that if you don't vote, you cannot complain about the 'party' elected by others to run the country. I went on to tell her about Mrs Pankhurst and the Suffragettes who demonstrated and marched in the streets, fought the authorities with some dying so that women could have the vote. My Aunt Eva was a suffragette.

"They were arrested and thrown into prison, and some would go on hunger strike and have to be force-fed through a tube which was humiliating and very painful."

Tina listened intently and nodded, but I didn't think I convinced her to go outside and place her vote. But still…it was getting late and we needed to get down the mountain again before dark as the roads can be very dangerous to drive on at the best of times.

Imbros Gorge

May

We had promised ourselves to do a walk down the Imbros Gorge last year and ran out of time. Preparations were made the day before, packing an overnight case and the rucksack for a mini holiday weekend away from home. The alarm clock was set for 7:00 am, so we could be out of the house early and on the road before the day got too hot.

This particular gorge is a popular one for summer tourists, therefore it is walked quite regularly so it would be a 'motorway of pedestrian traffic.'

Imbros Gorge is situated near Chora Sfakia and is the second most popular gorge walk after the famous Samaria Gorge on the island of Crete. It will take two or three hours to get there, hence the plan to stay overnight for bed and breakfast. From Rethymnon we drove on the National Road passing by the pretty fishing village of Georgioupoli and then further along to the Vrises turnoff heading due west. All we needed to do then was to follow the well-signed roads due south towards our destination.

Pulling into the large car park adjacent to a newly built hotel/taverna restaurant with its dining room partially suspended over the gorge and magnificent views across to the hills and mountains beyond. Our car was very dusty from the persistent strong winds blowing across from Libya to the South of Crete, leaving cloying yellow sand in its wake. We walked across the car park to speak to a young man who was lounging on the terrace waiting for customers, he said parking was free as long as we come in for a drink or maybe something to eat when we had finished our walk.

The sun was high in the sky when we set off in our sturdy walking boots with the rucksack packed with everything we would probably need. As we had predicted, we saw several groups of walkers in front of us advancing down the narrow dirt path towards the gorge entrance, disappearing into the comparative gloom where the enormous gorge walls enfolded and sheltered them from the searing heat of midday. We joined the queue at the little wooden booth to pay our four euro's entrance fee before proceeding. Unfortunately, it wasn't long before we were stuck behind a small party of six excited walkers, chattering and laughing loudly to each other as we all shuffled along. A few minutes later, we saw our chance to pass them on the dusty well-worn path covered with so many small stones as we slowly descended into the Imbros Gorge.

The magnificent high sides of the gorge rose up to meet us and we were embraced in the instant cool shade. The magnificent jutting rocks and pinnacles of the gorge sheltered us, plunging us into shadow for a short time. Any water from the winter rains had dried up, now there were just irregular indentations all along the wide riverbed. Sometimes the path ran alongside the riverbed avoiding many large boulders, other times we were walking along the bottom of the gorge. Unlike other gorges we have walked in the past, we had other hikers returning from the 'head' of the gorge so it became a 'high street' situation. Frequently standing to one side of the snaking dirt path to let others pass by our eyes were drawn to large clumps of Jerusalem sage which flower profusely in spring and early summer. Pausing now and then to let a steady stream of Imbros walkers pass us by, we enjoyed a cool refreshing drink of water standing under the ravage torn trees and surveyed our surroundings.

We were standing on a 'donkey trail' which heads towards Sfakia and is still beautifully cobbled in some parts, to lend some authenticity to the trail we see an old man sitting in the shade with his donkey tethered up nearby. The donkey had a very old wooden bucket saddle across her back, these are quite rare now and only seen in traditional museums in Crete. As we stood in the shade of a scrubby olive tree with its bare roots exposed – curling and twisting around some large smooth boulders in a snake-like fashion.

"It's like the League of Nations here," I whispered to Chris as a regular queue of Dutch, Swedish, German, English and Belgian people passed by. They either nodded and smiled or said hello, when there was a temporary break in the queue, I said I was quite exhausted answering them all.

"Maybe we should have walked this particular gorge either earlier in the year or towards autumn before the rains come," Chris replied.

However, we did enjoy talking to a nice middle-aged Canadian couple who were touring around the island for a few weeks in a hire car. They asked us about other gorges on Crete and places of archaeological interests, and we were only happy to oblige.

Pressing on again after our brief sojourn, we fell into step with the slow snaking procession of walkers who, like us, wished to stop now and then to take pictures or rest for a while in the shade and admire the views. We had been walking for about two hours now and the temperature was rapidly rising. The path narrowed somewhat and led us towards a huge boulder twelve or fifteen-feet high, worn smooth and shiny over centuries of torrential rainwater and snowmelt pounding over it. Turning down a sharp bend in the path, we looked in amazement at a natural narrow corridor ahead of us which was only 1.5 metres at its widest! The corridor acted as a wind tunnel and we lingered for a while to enjoy the pleasant cooling winds until we turned around and saw several walkers patiently waiting for us to move forward!

Another queue had formed in front of us now as other walkers had stopped to admire this unusual rock tunnel, some people had their arms outstretched and their palms touching the gorge sides, so we had to wait until they decided to move forward. Shuffling forward again a few minutes later, the path took us to where the gorge became wider and the backlog of walkers slowly dispersed way ahead. Setting off at a steady pace we talked about how many broken branches we had seen, along with various amounts of flotsam that had wedged into the rocks above our heads in the natural corridor. We could imagine the mighty floods in winter pounding down the gorge through the narrow corridor, bubbling and gurgling around the undulating bends and over the massive rocks and boulders with such a wild, natural force it would be very frightening.

"It must sound like a giant's bathwater when he pulls the plug out," I said. "I bet the noise must be deafening when the winter floods come down the gorge."

Passing an animal shelter and water trough to one side, we saw two local people selling cool drinks, raki and ouzo.

We were walking quite near the side of the gorge walls now when I stopped and pointed to a neat line of medium-sized stones firmly embedded along a carved-out shelf in the wall. The stones were about seven-feet-high from the bottom of the gorge, could it be that this line of stones was once the original gorge floor?

"It's a shame there aren't any coloured rock striations similarly to the ones we have seen in other gorges," I said, pausing for a moment to catch my breath whilst holding onto my sun hat. I craned my neck to look up at the blue peaks of the gorge, pointing up like sharp fingers at the deep blue sky. Maybe we have been spoilt walking in the lesser-known gorges such as Myli – with its lush vegetation and many different fruits of orange, lemon, fig and walnut trees. A natural riverbed flows all year from the mountains where little streams and waterfalls tumble over the smooth rocks. The old ruined village is being lovingly restored along with the stone watercourses, built long ago when The Myli Gorge (Mill Gorge) was an industrious and self-sufficient village. In recent years the pathway through the Myli has been re-built and restored, making it a lot easier for visitors to walk its length, and then rewarded with two delightful tavernas serving snacks and cool drinks. Or the magnificent Patsos Gorge which resembles an impressive Cathedral, or indeed the Prassenos Gorge which is still so untouched, you expect to see a dinosaur coming around the bend of the river bed any moment.

We eventually reached the Head of the Gorge with other walkers returning. There was a crudely made taverna with the sides made from old pieces of wood, the roof was thick bamboo canes providing shelter from the sun. One or two mature vines had grown through to give maximum leafy shade. The wooden terracing held a few tables and chairs, surrounded by a few large terracotta pots holding many colourful plants and herbs.

"No need to ask me if I want a rest and a drink," I said smiling at Chris as we approached two ladies sitting in the shade. The older lady jumped up and pointed over to one of the little wooden tables under the shady canopy. Smiling back at her I ordered drinks in her native tongue, she nodded and disappeared into the little lean-to kitchen.

Chris spotted the Canadian couple walking along the road towards the village and called out to them. "El-LA," (Hey there) I shouted cheerily peeping through the thick green shrubbery as they stopped and recognised us. "We may see you tonight in Anopoli village," she said, "we are on our way there now, if not it was nice to meet you both."

Returning to our table we saw the local taxi service by the side of the road, it turned out to be the old lady's husband business. We talked about the local people who are trying to make a living any way they can, with a sudden slump in the tourist trade during the time of the austerity measures.

"Have you seen what he is using as a taxi to drive some of the walkers into town? It's a big four-wheel drive pick-up." We watched two or three people climb into the back of the car and drive off in a cloud of dust. When our drinks came, the younger lady in the taverna had summoned up enough courage to ask another party of walkers, in broken English, if they wanted a taxi. One older lady did, she had walked down on her own and didn't relish the idea of having to walk all the way back in the soaring temperatures of mid-afternoon.

Suitably rested and refreshed it was time for us to walk back up the gorge, it was late afternoon, the intense heat was still beating down on us as we slowly walked back the way we came. I hadn't noticed a slight gradient when we walked down the gorge, but we certainly did on the return journey. To make the walk back as comfortable as possible we leant forward, folding our arms behind our backs as constant pools of sweat ran down our faces and into our eyes before dripping off the end of our nose! A constant warm trickle of sweat ran down our backs and soaks the tee shirts, forming pools in the waistband of our shorts. Uncomfortable wasn't the word for it! "I never realised you could sweat so much; it's making me feel faint again with the oppressive heat."

We had seen the lovely old donkey on our way down the gorge, tethered by a thick rope to a stake in the ground and sheltering under a large tree. The donkey looked well fed and cared for and further down the path sat the old goat herder on his well-worn padded chair outside a homemade hovel consisting of pieces of wood and large branches, making a crudely built canopy to shelter him from the heat of the day. He was lounging back on his chair drinking from a dirty chipped cup. His eyes latched on to us, his body was inanimate, it was just his bird-like eyes moving from left to right and watching us in idle curiosity as we passed by and said: "*Yasoo* (hello)." We learnt later he was appointed to help anyone in distress but also guard the impressive Venetian water cistern situated behind the ancient stone wall just beyond the man's hovel.

It was 5:00 pm when we arrived back at our car. I was feeling sick and dizzy with exhaustion as we changed out of our boots and walked across to the hotel/taverna for an iced drink. We had originally planned to drive over to Anopoli village tonight and find accommodation and walk another gorge the next day, but all I wanted to do was to lie down on a comfy bed in a cool bedroom and rest. But first, we needed to eat, we were both very hungry as our last meal had been an early breakfast. Perusing the menu, I selected the BBQed belly pork, with chips and veg. and Chris had lamb chops and breast of lamb, also with chips and veg. It looked delicious when the big guy brought our plates out and we tucked in, clearing our plates in next to no time. Chris ordered another drink for us and we sat looking out towards the undulating hills and the tops of Imbros Gorge as daylight faded revealing a spectacular sunset.

We were both feeling tired and aching from the day's walk, so we made enquiries for overnight accommodation then we would drive to Anopoli the next day. The taverna owner and his lovely elderly mother seemed genuinely pleased when Chris enquired about a room, he said: "It should be forty euro's but we could have a room for thirty-five euro's because we had bought a meal and drinks here." He led us up a flight of exterior stone steps leading off to a corridor that held three or four studio rooms. We were delighted with the room; we could see it had all been recently decorated and refurbished with a log burning fireplace at the far end of a large comfortable lounge. Centrally heated, it had a television, a new oven and a microwave in the newly built kitchen area. With the addition of a large modern tiled bathroom, we could not have asked for more. Needless to say, we both crashed out on the large comfy bed with a good book and a large carafe of their home-made wine and enjoyed the rest of the evening.

Sleeping soundly and totally refreshed we woke early next morning to the beautiful sounds of chattering birds and bright sunshine streaming in through the curtained window. Pulling the curtains back, we had a splendid view of the gorge and mountains in the distance. We wandered downstairs an hour later for some breakfast to be warmly greeted by the big guy and his lovely mother who began preparing our food in the kitchen. As he poured our freshly squeezed orange juice, he asked us if we had slept well. We said we had, he nodded and smiled before going to help his mother.

Chris whispered to me, "It must be a set breakfast," then the man appeared once more carrying two large plates of bacon and two fried eggs. Placing them down in front of us, he smiled again as he wished us – galee orexi (good eating). There was some white crusty homemade bread to dip into the large yellow yokes and on another plate was the old lady's homemade spinach parcels which she had made especially for us that morning. To finish off we were brought a steaming pot of strong black filter coffee.

"Well, that's set me up for the day," I said eating the last mouthful and patting my stomach. I was still stiff and aching from our strenuous walk down the gorge along with the oppressive heat and suggested we drive to the little fishing village of Choria Sfakion a few kilometres away. Settling our bill for the room and breakfast, imagine our surprise and delight when mother and son told us that our breakfast was included in the price of the room! With much handshaking, hugging and polite kisses on both cheeks from mum, we thanked them with the promise to return again.

Mid-morning, we arrived in Choria Sfakion, I remarked about the back windscreen being covered in a thick film of sand and dirt from the roads and the air. We strolled around the little harbour looking at many different coloured fishing boats along with their funny names, tied up alongside the jetty. A few fishermen were sitting on upturned fishing boxes over by the far side of the jetty sorting through their early morning catch. We thought we would venture nearer to see what they had caught, they were already in deep conversation, systematically cleaning a boxful of small octopus and squid. In the past, we have seen large amounts of octopus hanging out to dry on a rope line by the jetty, it looks peculiar and we haven't asked anyone why they do this, we think maybe they 'sun dry' and salt them to keep longer.

The aquamarine water of the Libyan Sea lapped against the concrete slope where fishing boats would either be launched or pulled out of the sea for repairs. With bright sunlight shining down onto the calm, tranquil waters of the sea in the harbour, it was casting a myriad of sparkling reflections and dancing on the water like a shawl of precious diamonds. We stopped walking for a little while, breathing in the clean salty air and enjoying the warm sun on our bodies.

The village reminded me of Agios Nicholias twenty-five years ago before it got overbuilt and commercialised. Peering over the jetty we watched shoals of tiny silver fish darting about in the sparkling sea. I remember throwing bits of bread to the fish after we had eaten our meal in one of the seafront restaurants. The fish were jumping out of the water in an attempt to get to the bread first. It was their Easter time – Paska, and the celebrations were exciting and memorable. We stayed in Agios Nicholias for the whole of Easter week and watched the story of Christ unfold, with fascinating celebrations in the little churches.

We passed by a few more fishermen as they busied themselves gutting and cleaning a large variety of locally caught fish, black sea bream, sea trout, sardines, red and black mullet etc. all caught from the seas surrounding Crete, so fresh and delicious! Slowly approaching the fishermen, they turned and looked towards us, their hard-working lives deeply etched on their faces; perpetually scorched by harsh weather conditions – hot sun and fierce strong winds and pounding rain, their faces told a story! As we passed by a gruff 'yassas' (hello) rumbled up from their barrel-shaped chests and then continued talking and cleaning their morning's catch.

Ahead of us and almost at the end of the jetty was a large building with a bleached and faded board outside advertising 'The Padi Diving Centre' several young men were in the process of either preparing to go diving or they had just returned from a morning's dive out at sea. Rubber wet suits, masks and a few pairs of large rubber flippers had been hung out to dry off in the warm sunshine. We had come to the end of the bay, and ahead were some stone steps leading up to a huge jutting overhang of rocks with a series of impressively coloured striations. Climbing up the steps to rest for a while, we sat on the top ledge out of the sun, I picked up a large piece of rock and examined it closely. It looked like a rich sandwich cake with a few coloured stripes running through it. It went from a deep burgundy colour to a reddish-brown, then deep green with bits of blue in it; eventually fading to a pinkish colour and then blending with the overall colour of creamy sandstone. Along with some quartz set in, the stone gave off a sparkling, shimmering effect, quite magnificent! And one to take back with me to place in my garden at Agia Triada.

The majority of rocks here are sandstone, probably because we are so near the Libyan Sea, but I can't say I have ever seen these particular markings before when we have been in Crete. The very delicate patterns on the rock looked like it had been painted with an artist's brush, it was so perfect.

Leaning back and relaxing in the cool shade for a while, we watched the guys at the Diving Centre messing around with their diving gear. Our sleepy eyes drifted over the expanse of the blue crystalline waters of the bay and to where fishermen were sailing their boats into the harbour. A few large seagulls circled over the bay, their sharp resonant calls splitting the quietude in the tiny fishing village. Tilting my face up to the sky, I closed my eyes – totally relaxed and happy to sit and dream for a while until the sun caught up to the cool morning shadows and chased them away, returning to hot sunshine once again.

"Let's go and find a nice shady taverna facing the sea and drink some freshly squeezed orange juice," I suggested, stirring myself into action again. We gathered our things together, I popped my latest natural treasure into the rucksack. Chris has got used to me collecting things of nature, he calls me a 'magpie'. Rocks, stones, shells and pinecones or anything else which takes my fancy go into the rucksack. When we go beachcombing, sometimes I collect the tiny colourful stones washed up along the seashore, it's like a button box of treasures. I then buy an A4 canvas and glue and make some lovely mosaic pictures for myself or my friends, I designed one mosaic in the shape of the Greek Eye. The stones and shells being collected when we drove from England to Crete via ferries, were from the beaches of Italy and Greece, the natural beauty of fauna and flora holds a great fascination to me and I cannot resist them.

Walking back around the bay, we chose a pretty little taverna at the other end of the promenade and facing a neatly tiled avenue of shops and tavernas, we were seated at a table by the water's edge. Sinking into the soft cushioned chairs to relax again under the shade of a large, colourful umbrella. We noticed the obvious absence of tourists around the village due to the severe austerity measures.

"It's only May, but in recent years the tourist trade here started around Eastertime and went right through until the end of September, although I don't know why they finish the holiday season so soon, a lot of retired people would come out in the winter months and stay if flights were available; but everything stops at the beginning of November until April the following year."

We sat for a while enjoying our refreshing drinks in a relaxed atmosphere and the warmth of the day, listening to the gentle lapping of the ebb tide and the distant cry of gulls.

"Ah! Bliss," I whispered to myself; I must have dozed off for a moment when Chris said, "I think we'd better make a move if you want to see the ruined fortress at Frangokastello further down the coast."

The car park had filled up considerably with two coaches pulling in as we were leaving. Following the coastal road running parallel to the sea, a warm gentle breeze was blowing into the car through the open windows as we sped along at a good pace towards our next destination.

How could the scenery change so quickly, from a pretty seaside resort to the stark barren waste it is now? I thought staring out of the car window.

An immense number of large rocks and stone laid in careless heaps all over the sparse landscape with thorny shrubs sprouting in between. "No lush grazing here." I thought how can farmers possibly make a living in such a harsh landscape. A few isolated dwellings were dotted about, providing shelter for the farmers and their sheep and goats, whether they lived here permanently or used the crude hovels on a daily basis we did not know.

We didn't see a soul until we approached the outskirts of Frangokastello, slowly descending on a steep helter-skelter road, leaving the moonscape terrain behind we looked down onto the small settlement below. The tiny hamlet had become popular due to the tourists' interest in the fortress ruins. Along with a pretty inlet bay surrounded by a narrow border of soft shingle, there was little else.

The huge square sandstone fortress, its four austere corners holding impressive round towers rose up to meet us as we advanced towards its impregnable walls. From a distance the fortress dominated the ugly landscape making the arduous journey worthwhile. On closer inspection our enthusiasm waned, we were disappointed to learn the fortress is just a mere façade and the interior was completely devoid of anything remotely interesting. The muted remains of an escutcheon depict the Venetian lion of St Mark. The fortress was built in 1371 A.D. to deter pirates and try to bring some order to Sfakia. A garrison was there throughout the Venetian and Turkish occupation, as with any ancient structure, there are folk law tales of martyrs, hero's and ghosts to try and entice the summer visitor to the fortress. Disappointed, but also glad we came we turned away having walked around its large square walls, to occasionally stand on tip-toe and peer inside through one of the oblong windows.

We were impressed with the huge heavy wooden door at the front of the fortress facing towards the sea, securely locked against pirates and many invaders down through the centuries. Massive iron nails had been hammered into the door itself for extra re-enforcement along with the huge iron hinges. Ironically, securely locked now against the curious tourists on a lovely summer's day!

We had seen what we came to see, although we did walk past a fairly new large taverna opposite the fortress which had probably been built to accommodate a regular stream of tourists who alighted from cars and coaches and spend their money.

"Too touristy for us," I remarked to Chris as we strolled by and saw thirty or forty holiday makers climb down from one of the coaches.

Sometime later, on our way home, we passed a sign indicating a WW11 Military Museum and decided to take a look. Following the turn off from the main highway it led us down a narrow single-track road until we came to a halt at the bottom of some steps leading up to a large old farmhouse. Climbing up the steep stone steps, there were many museum relics placed at each side of the path, including a field gun still in good condition. A pleasant young lady greeted us at the top step and in broken English asked us to follow her into the house. She said that the collection was started by her grandfather when he was just ten years old during the German Occupation and steadily increased the collection by her father who had received a lot more memorabilia over the years from various people.

It is indeed a fantastic collection from three generations of the family. The whole collection was not only Greek but German, English, Italian, Australian and New Zealand, every serving country that was there during the German occupation. Therefore, each country had a separate area in the large room, they covered the floors, walls and ceiling in a successful attempt to get everything inside. There were pictures, magazines, cigarette cases, shell and bullet cases, uniforms and helmets. Parachutes hung from the ceiling with their harnesses still attached. There was an immense and impressive amount of wartime hand guns and shotguns, knives and some improvised handmade weapons to try and defend themselves.

The young lady was very knowledgeable about the 'occupation' and didn't show emotion when she pointed to the section which held German Mauser guns and helmets, she told us that her family had lost some relatives during the occupation. Moving further around the room the young lady offered us a complimentary glass of raki before showing us the large collection of old magazines, some with strange propaganda pictures on the front covers depicting victory.

Having completed our interesting tour with her, taking us back to a time when this beautiful island was cruelly occupied and constantly under the threat of death, we warmly thanked her for her time. She pointed to a cardboard sign which read 'this is a Private Collection. We have no Funding from the Greek Government'. We were only too pleased to contribute some money and help with the upkeep of such a remarkable collection.

Chapter Nine

These halcyon days seem to roll into one round of walking, sightseeing, fun and adventure, sometimes we have to look at the calendar to keep track of the days!

Returning home one afternoon towards the end of May, having had a lovely day out and looking in our walks book for our next walking excursion, Chris drove around a sharp bend in the road, and before he could swerve to avoid some large stones that had fallen down during the winter storms from the overhang of rocks above us. I screamed in terror as the car shot up in the air and me with it, banging my head on the roof interior. The front passenger side wheel was not only punctured, but the rocks had bent the rim very badly. It was fortunate that we were very near home. As Chris was changing the wheel a local guy in a pickup truck slowed down and called out 'did we need any help'. Smiling and waving to indicate everything was okay we shouted back a 'thank you'.

The next day Chris took the hire car into two local garages to see if the wheel could be fixed. The car mechanics shook their heads and solemnly said, "It's kaput, take the car back to the hiring company." We were lucky to find the car hire shop a few kilometres from our villa, but unlucky when she told us that it was going to cost seventy euros to get it fixed, and maybe more when she saw the buckled wheel rim.

I got a bit upset and kept shaking my head and saying "*Oxi, oxi* (no, no)." She relented a little and said, "Maybe seventy euro's will be enough, but we should be more careful." We left the damaged wheel with her to be fixed and she told us to come back in two or three days when it would be ready.

"It's a lot of money out of our holiday funds," I said to Chris, feeling disappointed and upset. "With the price of hiring a car for a long period of time, coupled with the rising cost of fuel, it makes motoring expensive."

"We need a car to be able to see and do all the things you write about Patti, maybe we should think about buying a car and see if it works out a bit cheaper."

So, we did. We asked our dear friend Savvas first for his help and advice, he knew someone who owned a garage and sold cars and pickups here in Rethymnon.

"Shall I phone him and make an appointment?" he said.

We went with him to Yannis garage the day after that, we already knew what kind of vehicle we required. There she was! Waiting for us at the far end of the yard, an emerald green, Vitara 4x4. Yannis told us she needed some remedial work on her and a good clean. We bought our Sapphire for a fair price, and we have still got her based in Crete on Savvas land, some eleven years later. Of course, with any old girl she has her little foibles and hiccups, the luggage trunk doesn't open from the outside, we have to lean in and open the door from the back. An oblong piece of plastic has broken off, so we have a bit of trouble opening and closing the front passenger side window, but we love her with all her faults, I bought a few 'hippy stickers' when we went to Matala for a brilliant three-day rock concert on the beach. Everyone knows our car and they pip their horn and wave when we are driving Sapphire.

One morning towards the end of May, we thought we would go and visit our friend who lives in a cave in the Myli Gorge. We have walked this beautiful gorge many times but never tire of the splendid fauna and flora, the abundant wildlife, and the pretty streams and rock pools as we descend into the bottom of the gorge. Our friend has travelled all over the world backpacking and doing casual work, he is still a 'free spirit' even though he is on the wrong side of seventy years old. We have come to know him over several years now and we love to visit him, share a bottle of wine and talk about politics, world affairs or just some good old-fashioned gossip!

When we arrived at his elevated cave that day, it was very quiet and his front door was closed and locked up. We decided he must have gone down to Nadia and George's taverna, a few minutes' walk away. Don't be fooled into thinking he lives rough, he doesn't, he has everything he needs for day-to-day living including a wood-burning stove to keep him warm. He has fixed pipes along the roof of the cave and out through a hole in the top, the pipes hold the heat from the fire and makes for a basic style of central heating! His cooking facilities are a two-ring burner with a gas bottle attached, the gas bottles are delivered regularly to him from a friend who has a pickup. He has even fashioned a shower in the wooden lean-to next to the cave, warming a tank of water from the constant hot sunshine, it is piped along and connected to a showerhead, genius!

He has a comfortable bed and his books and music around him, he has all the fresh drinking water he needs just outside his door from the mountain snow melts and rain. He loves to re-cycle stuff and uses his old bicycle to get around and look for useful things other folks have thrown away. It could be some scruffy wooden dining chairs; he will mend and re-paint them to be used again. The best thing he does, in my opinion, is he looks for large pieces of old twisted vine roots broken away from the trees in the gorge, and with a lot of patience and hard work he fashions them into lovely works of art. We have one or two hanging on the walls in our villa, they look really nice.

As we approached 'The Banana Bar' Nadia was sitting with Yeorgi under a large palm canopy outside the door of the taverna with our friend seated at a table nearby. Soon as she saw us, she jumped up and rushed over to welcome us with big bear hugs and lots of kisses. We joined our friend who was sitting near a small plantation of banana trees, growing quite happily near the river bed. Nadia disappeared into the kitchen to bring food and refreshments out to us, and we relaxed into the peaceful quietness of the leafy gorge.

The low hum of conversation was punctuated now and then as we listened to the birds singing, bees humming and the soft tinkling of crystalline water flowing over smooth rocks and coloured stones on its journey to the sea. Yeorgi saw us admiring the large bunches of ripe bananas on the banana trees and jumping to his feet, he climbed up on a chair and deftly picked one of the bunches for us. He placed it on the table, giving a warm friendly smile, revealing a set of pink gums with only one or two tobacco-stained teeth remaining!

Nadia brought a delicious meze and cold drinks out for us, and we spent a lovely afternoon sitting in the shade of the banana trees, eating and drinking Nadia's home-made food and talking ten to the dozen. Although our hosts cannot speak English, with some help from our friend and my limited Greek, there was a lot of fun and laughter, sometimes gesticulating to make a point.

One of Nadia's cats had recently given birth to four cute kittens, we watched their antics as they climbed and tumbled over each other in delightful play. Chris took some photographs of Yeorgi posing outside the taverna door with my floppy sunhat perched on his head, manically grinning with his pink gums exposed and his remaining teeth like a 'row of condemned houses'. Not to be outdone, Nadia took my hat off his head and plonked it on her own at such a comical angle coupled with a silly grin, we fell about laughing as more funny pictures were taken.

Hooting with laughter she asked me to show her the photo's we had taken, before breaking into another wave of howling laughter. Waving to Yeorgi to come and take a look she proceeded to do a silly skipping dance round and round the tiled floor until she trod on the dog and collapsed exhausted into a chair – breathless!

"Oh, Nadia! I shouted; you are a goon." That set her off again, she caught hold of me and did a fast waltz round and round until I breathlessly begged her to stop. All too soon the lengthening shadows turned our funny memorable day into early evening as we told our friends it was time to go. Nadia pulled a sorrowful face whilst Yeorgi cut another bunch of bananas and wrapped them up along with some sweet cake which Nadia insisted we took with us as well for the journey home.

"We will come back again soon," we promised our friends as we walked back towards our car and made our way home. It was the end of a very memorable and happy day, but we knew there would always be a lot more to come in the future.

The next day we went to our local taverna to say goodbye to some friends, it is one of our favourite places to eat. Stratos, the owner, is such a nice guy and treats Chris and me like a special friend. When we order a drink from him, he always brings us two or three dishes of homemade mezethes with no extra charge. Stratos speaks quite good English but he talks very quietly and with our advancing years we cannot always understand what he says. When we first began to go into the taverna, shortly after we bought our villa in 2008, we thought his name was Stavros and addressed him as such, although he did tell Chris when he was ordering our drinks that his name was Stavos! Chris came back shaking his head and whispered to me that Stavros has just told me his name was Stavos, I think! "You know how quietly he speaks." So we began to call him Stavos. This went on for a few more weeks until an English lady – an ex-pat told us that his name was Stratos!

I started laughing and said, "Oh Really! We have been calling him Stavros and then Stavos for a few years, no wonder he keeps looking at us in dismay." We all saw the funny side of it and had a good chuckle. When we spoke to Stratos again a few days later, we apologised to him and said we had just found out his true name and we were sorry for the misunderstanding. He looked at us both and in a considered voice said "It's okay," and a big beam came on his face.

Later in the afternoon, I suggested we go for a nice walk along the pretty promenade at Rethymnon. It seems to be a regular pastime for the local people to 'promenade' on a Sunday and meet up with friends and family for a drink or a meal. The weather was still very changeable with a lot of clouds making the day dull, but warm and pleasant. We strolled along the promenade with many others going the same way, by the side of a beautiful clean beach and enjoying a fresh warm breeze blowing in from across the sea. It was still early in the season, with only a few beaches and souvenir shops opening their doors to sell colourful beach towels, sarongs, buckets and spades, sunhats and various creams to control the increasing heat of early summer sunshine. A few holidaymakers were sitting on brightly coloured deckchairs, completely engrossed in a good book, or stretched out under a large umbrella – totally relaxed. No matter what month of the year we come, we always see some brave individuals swimming in the sea, we have actually seen a few revellers around Christmastime, January and February!

The promenade gently arcs around to pass the pretty marina, where many large and small boats are tethered by rope to a large iron ring; cemented in the broad walkway. Many colourful fishing boats are moored up alongside, and one or two larger pleasure boats are also there to take tourists out into the deeper waters. There are also a few boats that can be hired by the skipper to take a party of people out for the day on a fishing trip. They also have two wooden Pirate ships, similar to the ones you see on *'Pirates of the Caribbean'* – they do a roaring trade for enthusiastic youngsters, and look quite magnificent when they sail out of the harbour into open waters. At the far end of the walkway, there is always one or two very large and expensive privately owned yachts, we love to go and admire them and see which country the yachts are registered to when we visit Rethymnon port.

We walked to the very end of the marina and looked out over the narrow strip of water to see several local children either sitting on some rocks in the sunshine or taking a cooling dip in the shallows. Their screams of laughter rang out across the golden sandy beach, in stark competition with the seabirds calling out over the calm blue waters of the Mediterranean.

"Oh, this is lovely," I remarked tilting my face up to the warm sunshine. We continued our walk along the promenade and eventually reached the old town to take shelter amongst the ancient high sided Venetian walls. We chose a pretty little Italian taverna to rest for a while under the dappled shade of ancient hanging vines.

The next day we rose quite early before the sun got too hot, and did some little jobs in and around the villa. Chris likes to take an early morning swim in the pool before breakfast, and he usually has the company of many beautiful swallows who dip and dive into the pool for a splash and a drink. They are quite amazing to watch, and when we stand quietly nearby, they come very close to us so we can see their beautiful markings. One or two nesting pairs have built their home under the stone archways of the villas, we look forward to watching them flying in and out with food for their noisy brood who chirp so loudly, opening their little bright yellow/orange beaks for more food.

I suggested having a walk after breakfast before the day got too hot to do anything strenuous. We could do a circular walk up through the olive groves and along the new road and back down again before breakfast. With only tee shirts, shorts, hat and walking boots we set off to do the short but pretty walk from home and into the foothills of the Psiloritis Mountains. The single-track road deteriorated rapidly as we made a steady climb up the steep, rocky road, running through the immaculate olive groves. Slowly passing the little turkey farm to our left we spoke about the old farmer talking to his charges last Christmas as if they were his children; muttering and clucking at them all with great affection. Suddenly there was a loud cacophony of clanging bells along with loud bleating, as a stampede of around eighty sheep came thundering down the narrow track road kicking up clouds of dust and stones in their path. The farmer was in the process of moving them further down the road to some new pastures after being milked earlier that morning. Tucking ourselves into the very edge of the dusty road, we stood still and quiet so as not to frighten them into charging off in the opposite direction. A few ewes hesitated for a moment and stopped to stare at us with their strange eyes. Then leaping forward at a standing start, they rushed past us, some of them jumping high in the air to try and catch up with the flock.

As we approached the top road, the scenery opened out into bare heathland, with a few wind-torn trees and thorny scrub dotted thereabouts, resembling in part, our bleak moorlands of England. I remarked to Chris that the ewes wouldn't get much sustenance from grazing up here because parts of the heath resembled a ravaged moonscape. As we levelled out and continued our walk, we were approaching the very end of the little gorge running alongside our villa and out to sea in Rethymnon town. We stood admiring the breath-taking views beyond, dotted with wild olive trees, yellow gorse and wild fennel, many as tall as myself. Large clumps of wild herbs were growing quite happily in and amongst the large rocks and scrubland. A cooling breeze blew down the gorge from the sea, gently stroking a variety of flowers and herbs and filling our nostrils with a pleasantly pungent aroma. Our dear friend Maria, who lives with her husband George near our home, is very knowledgeable of the culinary wild herbs and plants, it is such a pleasure to go with her when she collects them from the fields and hedgerows to use for either cooking or medicinal purposes.

We stopped for a while to try and identify some herbs, there was sage, lemon mint, coriander and many others we did not know, but they gave off a delicate fragrance when we rubbed the leaves with our thumbs. We turned down the new road and past the newly built petrol station advertising the cheapest petrol and diesel on Crete. At this time, both Crete and England are in the middle of a recession and with worse to come.

There is a little resident living in our villa at the moment, it is quite a large pale brown lizard about five inches long. I saw it creep into the folds of the voile curtains in the bathroom last night, probably came in through the open window. I was in the process of drying my hair and saw him out of the corner of my eye, he quickly disappeared up the wall and hid in the open wooden beams of the ceiling. Always welcome! Both lizards and geckos are harmless and will eat mosquitoes and other bugs which venture into the villa.

As we turned up the road for home, we heard the voice of a woman shouting "El-LA" coming from the villa further down. It was Mrs Smiley! As we looked across, she waved her hand to come over to her. She doesn't speak a word of English and she talks so fast in her native tongue I find it hard to catch what she is saying. On this occasion, when she had flung her arms around us with hugs and kisses, she motioned us to wait and disappeared into her home, coming out a few moments later, she presented us with a big bag of freshly laid eggs from her hens. More hugs, kisses and thanks were exchanged and we went on our way. We are not sure of her first name, but she has the biggest smile which lights up her lovely face, so the name has stuck.

Climbing up the steep winding road and past our friend's farm, we see George and Maria sitting on their little terrace having coffee with Maria's cousin Costa. When they see us, Maria gets up and welcomes us to come in and drink coffee. George gets up and with a big grin, he hugs and slaps Chris on his back, the typical way Greek men greet each other as friends, and then kisses me on both cheeks. Costa also gets up to greet us and pulls two chairs out for us to sit. We spend the next hour or so laughing and chatting over coffee and the delicious home-made Cretan food Maria had made. As we take our leave Maria, tells us to wait a moment and a few minutes later she comes out with a bag full of fruit and cakes!

Returning home, we remarked how kind and generous the Cretan people are, very humbling indeed!

Just outside the patio door from the lounge area, we have three mature olive trees which Chris has cut and shaped into splendid private hedging, screening us from the villa next door. Over time we have planted many brightly coloured geraniums from tiny cuttings I have picked on various walks. They have matured into lovely healthy plants and grow very tall over the summer months, resembling small trees. The large flower heads grow as big as a soup bowl and consist of white, pale pink, salmon pink and pillar box red. We also have a couple of mature rosemary shrubs which are sun-loving and produce a mass of tiny purple flowers, sometimes I cut a big bunch and hang them over the front door to enjoy their heady perfume. We also have three lemon geraniums the locals call 'Barbarossa' after the famous pirate, they produce deep purple flowers, the leaves are a similar shape to a maple leaf and you can cut these and use them in a salad.

We have promised our cave-man friend we will bring some unwanted clothes and household goods for him to take to the tabletop sale in Pigi, they raise funds for cat rescue on the island. A pretty little migratory bird flew in through the open patio doors and landed on my colourful Indian patchwork wall hanging, chirping loudly and somewhat distressed he tried to escape by flying into the closed window a couple of times before realising I had opened the other side of the patio door for him to escape. I don't like birds coming into the villa, either down the chimney or through the window and doors which they seem to do quite regularly. It is deemed very unlucky and I am superstitious.

Outside, our resident praying mantis is sunning himself on one of the deep yellow perfumed roses just outside the patio door. He is sitting squarely inside the very heart of one of the open flower heads, his bulbous eyes slowly follow me as I tiptoed past to hang some washing out to dry. I stood watching him for a while as he rocked from side to side on the upturned petals, and venture nearer to get a closer look at his perfectly formed body. Our 'new friend' has been with us for a few days now, eating the aphids and greenfly off the roses, we have begun to look for him every morning to see if he is still outside the villa. He loves the sunshine and spends all day following the sun as the lengthening shadows fall across the roses. One morning I was sitting reading on the patio and he slowly climbed down from his perch to visit me and sit for a while near my feet. I stopped reading and looked down at him looking up at me with his head on one side, I spoke gently to him for a while until he returned to his usual perch. Maybe he is a reincarnation of someone I have known in life from another time? I'd like to think so!

I related my extraordinary experience to Chris on the way to visit our friend, he laughed and said he would have liked to have seen him. It was late afternoon when we arrived at our friend's cave-dwelling, he was pottering around outside watering his tomato plants and flowers which he had planted just below the concrete steps leading up to his home. He's such a lovely guy and very interesting to talk to having travelled all over the world during his lifetime. We had a nice drink and chat on his terrace and sipped some crystal-clear spring water from the Myli Gorge which he had bottled that morning from the old stone watercourses nearby. He was very pleased with the gifts we had brought for the sale and in return, he gave me one of his books to read later. As we sat with him in the coolness of his cave home, I couldn't resist glancing around at his eclectic collection of quirky object d'art. He told us about various people he had met whilst living here in Crete over the last 25 years which we found interesting. I would love to write his 'life story' but when I mention it, he clams up and shakes his head slowly saying, "There is nothing much to tell." We think otherwise but we care enough about him to respect his wishes.

Chapter Ten

May

It started blowing hard outside last night and woke us both up, Chris got up and brought the outside door curtain in which was constantly banging on the front door, he said there is a hot wind blowing up from the South of the island, it continued all the next day bringing fine yellow sand with it and covering everything outside. Trying to clean it away is a feat in itself, if you have ever tried to get rid of concrete dust it's just the same problem, the more you wipe the worse it gets.

We made plans to go away for a couple of days to Lasithi Plateau and do some walking, staying overnight in a local taverna. Later that day we went to visit our old friend Georgia, who has a taverna in the tiny hamlet of Agrimouri situated above the beautiful fishing village of Georgiapoli. She told us, she has never left Crete and never travelled any further than Chania on the bus to visit her sister. She married a local man who was cruel and beat her constantly; now he is dead and good riddance – BAH! "He is over there," she told me pointing to the church graveyard.

The magnificent views of the Lefka Ori (White Mountains) come into view as we leave the pretty fishing village of Georgiapoli behind and drive over the narrow bridge where many ducks and geese hide amongst the reed beds below and out of the sun. The arrow-straight road ahead is elegantly framed by a series of mature eucalyptus trees with their pale leafy green branches cascading down dramatically over the roadside, their creamy coloured bark peeling like a snake shedding its skin. As the road narrows, we start to climb, snaking around many small olive groves and villas until we pause to glance across at the smoky blue range of the Lefka Ori in the far distance, some still with snow in the crevices and gullies; glinting like icing sugar in the afternoon sunlight. Cotton wool balls of low cloud float and swirl around the sharp peaks, giving a dramatic overall effect as my eyes drift down to a small herd of sheep grazing far below, so tiny they look like a child's miniature farmyard animals.

Parking the car at the far end of the village opposite the church, we look at the magnificent views beyond and say a villa would be just the thing on this very spot! Immediately to our left we look towards an olive grove on a gentle slope overlooking the pretty bay of Georgiapoli and owned by Georgia's family. Ahead is the dramatic range of mountains, and just below a patchwork of carefully tended olive groves and ploughed land with a scattering of farms reminding us of the lush pasture lands of England.

Sitting on the rickety chairs under Georgia's very old walnut trees on the patio, their ancient arms spreading out to embrace the hot sun and welcome the cooling winds from the sea. Georgia fussed and grinned, patting and hugging us like long lost friends, then brought us some of her delicious homemade retsina and meze on a tray along with two glasses. "Full to the brim," Chris muttered. "How she manages to walk all this way across to us without spilling a drop is beyond me." "Years of practice," I replied holding my breath until she set the tray down in front of us. We settled back in the shade of the trees to enjoy our wine and watched Georgia come over to us with a large brandy in her hand.

"Just a small one," she said glancing across to us and grinning as we stared back at her open-mouthed. "If that's a small one, Chris said I wonder what she would class as large." I nodded in amusement and enjoyed some small talk with her in my then, limited knowledge of the Greek language. If I open my little phrasebook, Georgia will wave it away. "Just speak or gesticulate, that way you will learn." I must admit in the early days of learning she did help me a lot and she had unending patience, but as she gets older, she ends up falling asleep in mid-conversation, always reminding me of the dormouse in the teapot in Alice in Wonderland books.

About an hour later, a young male tourist came strolling by so we invited him to join us for a drink and something to eat to help bolster Georgia's income. He introduced himself as Hansel, an artist from Amsterdam; who could speak fluent Greek and English. He went on to tell us he was backpacking around the island and his base was in Chania. Georgia became upset with his 'intrusion' because he was excluding her from the conversation to talk to us. She started pulling faces and tutting loudly then gave up and nodded off again to be woken up later by a battered pickup truck with a very large loud speaker announcing he was selling fresh oranges. Muttering inaudibly, she jumped up and went over to buy some and I did the same, we came back with a huge bag of juicy oranges for just five euros each.

As the afternoon progressed Georgia seemed to have taken an instant dislike to Hansel and kept pulling faces at him and waving her hands to shoo him away. The more she did it the more he laughed, and told us she thinks I have the evil eye and for me to go away and not come back! We left Georgia when the sun began sinking slowly behind the silhouetted mountains, the magnificent evening sky vivid with slashes of blues, reds, crimson and gold. We gave Hansel a lift back down the steep hillside and into Georgiapoli, where he caught his bus back to Chania.

To round off the lovely day, we called into our local taverna and Stratos made us some delicious hot Cretan food for supper, and together we talked about seeing Georgia again and made plans for our mini walking holiday.

The first time we ever met Georgia was on a very wet rainy day after we had done a circular walk which is situated in the hillsides above her taverna. We were wet through and cold, so we welcomed her warm room and cheery disposition. Peeling our layers of wet clothes, she brought us a jug of red wine and beckoned us to sit down. A few minutes later, she came out of the kitchen with some hot food, it was a hearty chicken casserole probably from one of her chickens nearby, and we think it must have been her dinner, but she gave it to us instead. At that time, I didn't speak much Greek and Georgia doesn't know any English but for an hour or so we chuckled at her antics, hiding our faces so she couldn't see us laughing at her just in case she got upset.

She watched us eat every mouthful like a mother hen, nodding and smiling as we hungrily tucked in, and when we had drunk the wine and cleared our plates, she brought another jug of wine, then patted me and grinned. Sitting back in our chairs, warm, full of food and wine and content. We watched Georgia get up, taking great pains to lift a wooden chair before selecting a light bulb off the counter, coming back to the chair she looked across at us and attempted to lift one leg to climb up. Moans and groans followed with Georgia glaring at us until Chris took the bulb off her to do it himself. Constantly patting him and muttering to herself, Chris reached up to fix the lightbulb in place, it was the old screw-type fixture and as Chris quickly began to screw it in; Georgia shrieked at the top of her voice, "Sega, Sega" (slowly, slowly) she boomed out and began flapping her arms around like a demented windmill.

Drama over and Chris and Georgia returned to their seats to sit for a while in front of the fire and the TV turned down low, then Georgia started fiddling with what looked like a makeup bag and pulled out a lipstick. She started pulling at the top of the lipstick, tutting and muttering to herself and eventually looking across at us again! "Oh, ho, now what," I exclaimed laughing. She looked pleadingly at me, so I reached across and took the lipstick, after several tugs the top wouldn't budge and I passed it over to Chris who did the same, nothing! "I think someone was having a joke with her and has superglued it to the bottom half," I said, watching Chris.

"Oxi, Georgia," (no, Georgia) Chris said shaking his head. She mumbled something and threw it back into her makeup bag in disgust.

We had lots of fun and good experiences with Georgia over the years, I have written about her in my other book. Just because she is such a lovely character her reputation has grown and she has many visitors from abroad to come and see her and enjoy her warm eccentricity.

A Poem for the Summer Time

By: Paul, Laurence Dunbar

When summertime has come, and all
The world is in the magic thrall
Of perfumed airs that lull each sense
To fits of drowsy indolence;
When skies are deepest blue above
And flowers a flush-then most I love
To start, while early dews are damp
And wend my way in woodland tramp
Where forest rustle, tree on tree
And sing their silent songs to me

Where pathways meet and pathways part
To walk with Nature heart by heart
How swiftly glide thy days along
Adown the current of the years
Above the rocks of grief and tears

Tis wealth enough of joy for me
In summer time – to simply be.

Chapter Eleven
Walking on Lasithi Plateau

We had promised ourselves to do a two-day walking holiday on the beautiful Lasithi Plateau with bed and breakfast, in one of many quaint villages surrounding the verdant plateau.

The plateau itself is divided into oblong pastures, and planted with many neat rows of vegetables, fruit trees and well-tended vineyards. Craggy mountains provide a circular backdrop to shelter the rich pasturelands from harsh weather during wintertime, although when the snow melts from the mountain tops the plateau is usually abandoned by the local farmers as the icy water rushes down to flood the plateau for a few weeks making life there inhabitable. Then, most of the inhabitants will go back to their family homes for the winter months until springtime.

Today, the sun is shining brightly in a vivid Mediterranean blue sky with some snow still visible on the very tops of the mountains giving a layered look of undulating hills, massive rocks and boulders, gorges and caves. In the foreground, there are many olive groves and miles of flat green land stretching out into the distance. Generous scatterings of wild, blood-red poppies nod their heads in the warm breeze as we walk by on one of the many single-track paths that lead the way through the plateau itself.

One or two plots of uncultivated land have reverted back to nature, they have many beautiful yellow, purple and white flowers growing in tangled profusion, reminding us of a Monet painting.

At this time of year, the farmers who tend their olive groves are busily clearing the land of debris that has collected during the winter months underneath the olive trees and then plough to refresh the soil. We see many old tractors and antiquated farm machinery, still in good working order, with some passed down from the previous generation of the family.

With the coming of 'austerity measures' in Greece and other E.U countries, a land tax has been recently introduced. Previously, many small plots of land, have been left fallow and unused, they are now having to pay an annual fee to the government. In some ways, it's a good thing, as we now see the once derelict land being planted out with crops and olive trees in the recent months to bring some income.

On route to the plateau, we drove into the bustling town of Kastelli to rest a while and stretch our legs. We found a delightful taverna on the main street and fell into conversation with a pleasant elderly lady and her brother, who owned the taverna. I concentrated very hard to speak to them in their native tongue, and I was rewarded later with a compliment from her brother on my command of the language, which pleased me a lot. The old lady beckoned us to come and look at their pretty garden at the back of the taverna when I told her I loved flowers and gardening.

"It's all my brother's work," she proudly told us, smiling back at her brother who nodded in agreement. It was indeed a quiet little oasis, with a beautifully paved courtyard set in a high walled garden and hidden away from the view of the busy town. Two large mature trees cascaded down, providing leafy shade in the summer months and a home for many little birds who sing in the canopy. Set into the far wall was a lovely old stone well complete with a large lion head spewing clear spring water into a trough below. An avenue of many and varied brightly coloured plants and shrubs framed the surrounding walls and a carefully positioned table and chair for the old lady and her brother to use in the hot summer evenings – it was a joy to see.

We returned inside the taverna, and her brother pointed to the magnificent natural stone inglenook fireplace he said he'd built, around the time of the fountain in the garden. He was indeed an accomplished stonemason, and we thought the fireplace and the beautiful garden looked like it had been there forever. We said our goodbyes and returned to the car and drove out of the village. Ascending a series of tight corkscrew bends on the uneven road, we saw a brown tourist sign advertising an important Minoan settlement at Karphi.

Putting our walking boots on we walked down to where the narrow path would lead us over to the ruined village beyond. Entering into a large expanse of carefully tended olive groves, we made our way along a series of dusty dirt paths which divided each grove, one from another. A quiet hush descended, broken only by the sweet sound of bird song and the low hum of large honey bees collecting pollen from the wildflowers nearby. Eventually, we came to a lovely ruined church which was said to be 200 years old, built on a high promontory with a 360-degree view.

Unfortunately, as we turned the large metal ring to open the heavy wooden door, it was locked against us. We have noticed more and more places of worship now lock their doors for security against theft. We remember a time when we first visited Greece and their islands, no door was locked against the traveller. It is sad to learn from our Greek friends, there have been numerous thefts from museums and churches.

Retracing our steps down the dusty road we call out a cheery 'Yasso' to an old farmer who was tending his vines. His wiry body was bent forward, systematically pruning his trees to encourage the goodness to return to the main body of the vine, then the tiny bunches of grapes will 'set' and mature with the help of the hot sun and refreshing rain bringing a good harvest of juicy grapes later in the year.

We eventually reached another old church built on the usual high ground, it would probably be locked but we decided to climb up and admire the magnificent views down the valley, and in the distance a cluster of buildings. Our patience was rewarded when the ruins of a Minoan/Roman settlement came into view. Steeped in ancient history and as yet to be excavated, it is considered one of the most important archaeological sites to date. We came across the remains of crudely built single-storey dwellings, founded in twelfth century B.C. the Minoan refugees were now fleeing from the advancing Dorians.

Around 3,000 inhabitants had lived in the ancient town of Karphi, the high inaccessibility provided a great defensive and coupled with the fertile plateau nearby, successfully growing a large number of yearly crops for food. We wandered around the site for quite some time, looking and contemplating, discussing and weighing up just what life would have been like for the people all those years ago. We always love to do this and try to discover as much information as we can and read about it later when we return home.

We drove onto our next destination, down to the village of Psychro to look for accommodation for the night. Passing through a few tiny hamlets on the broad circular road which runs around the base of the plateau I couldn't see anything suitable to book in for the night, so we decided to ask someone at the next taverna we came to. A very eager to please elderly lady came out to greet us, and hearing our request she asked us to wait whilst she spoke to her husband. He told us his friend had a place we could stay overnight and he would telephone him. By the time we got to see the room it was almost dark, we were tired and hungry and in need of a shower and something to eat. The small, dirty and damp room was accepted by us without any quibble. Imagine my dismay when I turned the shower on and received an icy cold blast of freezing mountain water and no promise of piping hot water to warm my aching bones!

"Aahhh!" I shouted at the top of my voice. "The water is freezing Chris."

"Get dried and dressed and I'll go across to the house and tell them," he called back.

Returning a few minutes later, he found me huddled under the blankets on the bed trying to get warm, Chris said "They will put the emersion heater on and we should have hot water in about twenty minutes."

The shower water was just about warm over an hour later and we resigned ourselves to having the quickest shower ever and then find somewhere to eat before we died of hunger. We thought we may as well eat at the taverna we had seen earlier, remarking on the lack of locals and tourists when we walked into the large empty room devoid of other diners.

We certainly cheered up when the kind lady brought us a veritable feast to the table. Our starter was shredded goat meat with a bowl of fresh crispy salad followed by large juicy slices of BBQed belly pork, homemade chips and vegetables. I groaned inwardly as our genial host then brought us a complimentary sweet dish of almonds and honey along with a small jug of raki for the table. "Blimey they like their food over here," I whispered to Chris when she returned to the kitchen, "My poor stomach, I can hardly move after eating all this food."

"Well, she's done us proud Patti, we can't grumble at this meal, a delicious home-cooked dinner at a very reasonable price," Chris replied.

Returning to our accommodation for the night, we slept soundly and woke refreshed the next morning for good days walking.

The early morning sun shone through the grubby thin curtains to herald a fine but cold morning. We got dressed and packed our overnight case, driving to the village Agios Georgios nearby and ordered two large cups of coffee at a pretty café overlooking the square and the junior school. We were waiting for the sun to gain strength, we made the mistake of leaving our warm clothing behind, not realising the early morning temperatures here would be colder than along the coastline. We would remember next time we would bring warm fleece and long trousers.

In our walking book, it says we are 1,800 metres above sea level, so the brisk morning chill will always be apparent through the summer months.

Sipping our hot coffee, our attention was drawn to a small group of young Albanian men leaning against the wall in the square and waiting to be chosen to do a day's casual labour on the land. A few minutes later, a local farmer drew alongside the group and pointed to just one man indicating for him to climb on the back of his tractor.

As the crisp morning air gave way to the soft warmth of early summer, we strolled around the pretty working village, ending up amongst a few derelict properties. We guessed this would once have been the original village and maybe they would have become derelict once the tenants had died. Although one or two looked like they were being used as a squat, we peered in and saw some rough bedding, shoes and other domestic detritus were strewn around the dirt floor interior, maybe it was the home of the Albanian men we had seen earlier.

Returning to the car we drove on to explore the next village and passed the remaining group of Albanians who hadn't been picked for work that morning, they were now lolling against one of the derelict villas talking amongst themselves. It must be a hard life for them here, never knowing where the next meal will come from, but we don't know what their living conditions must have been like before.

The scenic short drive took us into the larger village of Agias Constantino's where small groups of visitors were strolling around in the early afternoon sunshine, we parked the car and walked up the length of the attractive village until we saw an old wooden signpost with the legend FARANGI (gorge) pointing to the far end of the village. Putting our walking boots on, we walked down the narrow dirt path away from the crowds. The lush green countryside immediately opened up to us as we passed by a substantial amount of healthy crops growing in rich loamy soil in many large tilled fields. I pointed up to a huge stone domed hill sharply rising up in the cornflower blue sky and remarked to Chris 'what a strange landmark it was and how out of place it looked'.

The narrow dirt path slowly wound through the crop fields as we climbed higher, taking us nearer to this oddly shaped landmark. Then, thundering towards us there must have been around 200 freshly milked sheep, a grey dust cloud swirling around as they excitedly leapt forward to get past us, with others curiously eying us up before increasing their gallop again. Bleating loudly, they continued their journey down to a nearby field and grazed once more on lush pastureland.

"Well, you could get killed in the stampede," I said laughing as we continued along the dirt path. Chris nodded sagely and replied "Do you remember that time when we went to visit our Cretan goat herder, and he asked me if I would like to try and milk one of his goats? He said he'd put me with a docile one to get some practice, but I ended up getting kicked, the milk bucket went flying and the goat ran off."

Coming to a recently built large reservoir situated just below a rocky outcrop providing irrigation to the local vineyards and crops, we crossed a concrete bridge and passed through two metal gates into a beautiful gorge stretching out before us in the distance. We followed the familiar 'red dot' walker's sign which had been carelessly splurged on a conveniently placed smoothly rounded boulder. The gorge itself was completely dry now being the end of May, but during the winter floods and ice melt it would have poured down from the high mountains and quickly fill up the deep gorge mouth. The water would rush over many rocks and boulders in the gorge ripping out overhanging trees and shrubs in its wake as the sheer force of the water would bubble and boil down to meet the larger stream beds and eventually run out to sea.

Evidence of some larger olive branches stripped bare of jagged tree bark and bleached white with the constant pounding of water are firmly wedged into the huge rocks above us. We walked on fine dark grit sand inside the gorge, constantly pulverised with the sheer force of water.

Walking for about an hour, we picked our way over some recently fallen rocks threatening to block our path. We proceeded slowly, with no alternative route other than climb over some large boulders which blocked the path, eventually reaching a small clump of trees further up the gorge. It was here we decided to stop the walk as the smooth boulders became much too large to climb over safely, along with their slippery surface we could easily have an accident. It is always with the utmost care when we walk in Crete, especially in gorges where the mobile signal is usually unavailable due to the high sided rock face. Several people have died in Crete in remote areas, in various gorges and the seas of Crete's. One unfortunate couple were walking in the Samaria Gorge and died through heat exhaustion when they ran out of water, their mobile signal didn't work due to the high sided gorge walls. The lady collapsed and died first; they found her husband a few kilometres ahead of her with a mobile phone still in his hand. The notorious 'rip-tides' are prevalent abroad as well as at home, sometimes it is too late to realise the sand beneath your feet is slowly moving and pulling you down.

On our return, we stopped to chat with three other walkers who asked us how far up the gorge went. We said we had been walking for over two hours, when we had got as far as the clump of trees then we decided to turn back because of the massive boulders blocking the path.

It was 3:00 pm when we returned to the village to rest and have an orange juice before setting off back home. It would be a three-hour journey and hoped we would get back before dark.

Later in May, we thought we would go and explore the newly built Potami Dam and read about the details of its magnificent construction.

"The Lake of Potami is shaped by the Potami Dam in Amari province, it was built in 2008, 25k south of Rethymnon. The lake has a capacity of 23 million cubic metres and is one of the most important wetlands in the Southeast Mediterranean, with many species of birds and animals being recorded in the area. The dam gathers water from the gorge of Patsos, the small valley of Pantanassa and the stream of Stavromana originating from Agia Fotini, just above the barrier you can still see the ruined Fort Koules."

In July, 2014 two firefighters saw a crocodile, two metres long on the shore! Various services tried to capture the lovely reptile but didn't manage to trap it. Sadly, the crocodile named Sifi, died in March, 2015 after an unusually bad winter by Cretan standards.

We spoke to our friends George and Maria about the crocodile, and George refused to believe Sifi ever existed but offered to take us there to take a look in the Potami Dam. I whispered to Maria on the way there to pretend we had seen it, just for some fun.

"Look Maria, there he is," I shouted excitedly, pointing to the sunlight shimmering on the lake.

"Oxi, this cannot be," George replied, shaking his head.

Maria added credence to our story by nodding sagely and confirming the story.

George flatly refused to believe a crocodile could live in the lake, so we all went home again. However, a few weeks later we watched some film footage of Sifi the crocodile which someone had filmed from a helicopter. We mentioned it to George and still, he refused to believe it, saying the film was fake! They never did find out who put poor Sifi into the Dam, one theory is it was a pet smuggled in when it was small and it got too big to handle as a pet.

We stayed in Crete that winter, we were snowed in for three days, never having seen snow come down so fast before, covering our garden and pool in a thick layer of soft white snow. Our friend Maria managed to wade through knee-deep to see if we had enough wood for the fire and enough food to see us through. The snow continued for a few more weeks, but not so bad we couldn't manage to get the car out and go shopping for groceries. We heard the snow had come right down to the water's edge in Rethymnon and the olive trees and palm trees had suffered extensive damage with the weight of snow! The Cretan people were astonished, and said 'they had never known Crete to have such a fall of snow before'. Many photographs were taken of the beach and promenade at Rethymnon, it was the topic of conversation all winter that year. A couple of weeks later when it was quite safe, we drove into the mountains to admire the 'winter wonderland' − it was truly spectacular, a few young families had the same idea. The young children were busy having snowballs fights and tobogganing down the sloping hillsides, enjoying the newly fallen snow which many had never seen before.

In the summer months, there is always a huge glut of fruit and vegetables, our friends are always generous with big bags of cherries, tomatoes, sweet grapes, lettuces, cucumbers, aubergines and oranges. We do not like to waste anything and only keep what we can eat, or make a Raki liqueur and the rest we offer to friends. Of course, our door is always open to adopted family and friends, so we end up sharing our delicious food and drink with them all. That is the Cretan way! And that is our way too!

One morning our neighbour brought us a large bag of juicy cherries, saying they had been picked earlier that morning from their friend's cherry orchard. She went on to tell us they were going to the christening of their grandchild, would we like to go with them? The child is usually two years old when they are christened. One year George and Maria invited us to attend their youngest grandson's christening and a celebration party later, we felt very honoured and immediately excepted.

The morning of the Christening saw us wearing our best clothes and walking down the lane to George and Maria's farmhouse, going with them in the car to the local church. Their youngest daughter, Georgia, sat with us to explain the christening ceremony as it slowly unfolded.

The ceremony is very strange to outsiders, the young child is carried into the church by the father wearing their oldest clothes. Then the God parents take all the child's clothes off and one of the three priests holds the child over a large stone font. He gently lowers the child into the warm Holy Water, totally immersing them three times and saying a prayer. By then the child is in such a state he or she is screaming the place down and asking for their parents, this is usually ignored by the priests and congregation, the completed ceremony is when the child is carefully dried by the God Parents on a table near the altar and then dressed in their new clothes bought especially for the occasion – the literal significance being 're-birth and new life'. Then the celebrations begin, and all the family and friends drive to a pre-booked taverna or restaurant, to eat and drink and dance and celebrate the newly christened child. It was a memorable day for us, a totally new experience, and something your average tourist or visitor would never see.

Chapter Twelve

We usually do our food shopping on a Thursday in the open market in Rethymnon town. The market opens for business at 6:00 am and finishes around 2:00 pm. It is all locally grown produce from the villages around as well as clothing, shoes and various complementary stalls. Situated in the centre of town on the car park, it is a very popular weekly market for locals and tourists alike.

The atmosphere was lively as we approached the market just before 11:30 am with the usual gypsy beggars lining the route along the road. A young woman sitting on the pavement dressed in old shabby clothes was holding her baby close to her chest with her hand outstretched for money she was muttering something inaudible to us as we passed by. As a rule, we do not give money to the beggars but one particular week when we were coming out of the market we saw an old man – a local Cretan man, badly crippled sitting on the floor and holding a dog-eared picture of his family. We approached him and bent down to meet his gaze, and said, "*Yasso,*" as Chris put a few coins in his box. His tired old face creased into a smile and thanked us then asked if we were '*Allemande* (German). "Oxi, Anglia (No, English)," I replied.

We usually walk from the marine car park through the centre of Rethymnon town and up to the busy open market which takes us a good half hour. Comparing fruit and vegetables first, we usually pick the same market traders who have become our friends, knowing we will get a good deal. Our favourite cheese stall is owned by two brothers who make all their own cheese in the Psiloritis Mountains. We moved on to purchase locally caught sardines for the BBQ. A huge bagful is handed to me by a crusty old seadog for just three euro's, what a bargain! Next, we buy salad tomatoes as big as small footballs, locally grown lettuce still with Cretan soil on them and the biggest spring onions you can imagine, just like small trees! We see homegrown leeks three feet long and the water melons are so big you need a hand cart to get them home. The taste of all the home-grown stuff over there is amazing and so healthy, no artificial crop spray, it's just how everything was grown when my father planted out vegetables in our large back garden after the War.

Purchasing some delicious juicy oranges from 'Georgios the orange man' for breakfast orange juice next day I began to load them into our rucksack whilst Chris paid him. He then tells Georgios we have a donkey now.

"You have a donkey here in Crete," he replies with his eyes widening.

"Yes," Chris replied nodding – "It's ME!".

Georgios face crinkled up and emitted a good belly laugh saying "Oh! That's a good one, You, are the donkey."

Returning to our car loaded up with fruit and vegetables we placed them in the cool box next to the frozen ice packs, the midday sun had reached its zenith producing a visible heat haze over the bay.

Scenic Drive and Walking in the Seaside Resort of Paleochora

Our journey will take us in a South West direction over the mountains towards the beautiful seaside resort of Paleochora. The rucksack had been packed the previous evening, so all we had to do was grab a quick cup of coffee and hit the road before 8:00 am, before the day got too hot.

Paleochora was originally known as Kastel Selinou – the castle of Selinos, and for much of its history was no more than that, a castle. Built by the Venetians in 1279, the fort was destroyed by Barbarossa in 1539 and never properly reconstructed even when the small port grew up beneath it. The ruins are still perched at the bulbous end of the headland now occupied by the settlement of Paleochora. With many beautiful bars and restaurants within the town, coupled with a lovely beach and crystal-clear sea it's an ideal place to visit and stay for a while.

The clouds were beginning to clear, revealing an attractive azure blue sky as we sped along the quiet road with warmth from the early morning sun through the car window. Through the village near our home, we pass by the little school where children are walking in single file along the road with their parents on their way to morning lessons, beginning early at 8:00 am.

Out on the National Road, we are heading in the direction of Chania. There is still quite a bit of snow on the Lefka Ori (White Mountains) even though it is almost the end of May, it is usually visible until June when temperatures soar and slowly the ice and snow melt filling the streams and river beds with deliciously clean fresh mountain water.

Speeding along down the main highway Chris pointed out a couple of sheep which had broken loose and were happily grazing alongside the fast-moving traffic. My attention was drawn to a very old and battered pickup truck with a lovely brindle and tan Alsatian dog in the back of the truck, just loving the cool wind blowing his fur, his ears flapping up and down and with his mouth partially open – he looked a comical sight.

Passing the turnoff for Suda Bay, there is an American naval base there as well as a large ferry port for cargo and passengers. An elegant cruise liner is berthed up alongside an impressive naval ship. There are also a few fish farms centrally placed in the bay with their large square net spread across the calm water and undisturbed by passing boats.

Our onward journey takes us through the winding road climbing up and up through the field after field of large healthy olive groves and vineyards until we see a bleached wooden sign indicating we are coming into 'The Martyred Village of Kako Petros (Dirty Peter) we didn't know then how the village got such a strange name but we did find out later that day.

We hear that the villages around the Suda Bay area were under siege when the Germans occupied the island. The local men of the village held the Germans back for three days until the allied soldiers could escape to re-group later, sadly all the men, women and children were brought out and shot in the village square in vicious reprisals, leading to the village being name 'Martyred' as a result.

The sleepy village of Kako Petros nestles at the head of a verdant gorge in a place that time forgot, pausing for a while to read the impressive monument set back from the road reading 28th August, 1944 and the names of the local men who had been killed in action in the 1941–45 war.

Leaving the village now, we follow the narrow snaking road to stop again and admire the magnificent views of wild rugged mountains and the gorge below us, with some reminding us of Scotland or Yorkshire in England. Some land had been carefully ploughed around the strips of olive groves, exposing pale golden sand-like soil with the remains of last year's dead grass it looked from a distance just like a field of wheat. The grey slate-coloured rocks rose sharply up exposing narrow goat tracks running alongside their base, tempting keen walkers to pull on their boots and explore its length. At the very bottom of the gorge, we can see the dried-up river bed cutting through the lush unkempt shrub growth giving some shade to either goats or walkers.

We were very tempted to abandon our original plans and climb down to do a lovely walk there, but after some initial discussions, we agreed to keep it in mind and come another day. This isn't the first time we have driven out in the car and spotted other likely walks, Crete is blessed with so much to see and do. We have been coming to Crete and the Greek Islands for many years and still keep finding new places to visit.

The gorge is named 'The Gorge of Masavlia' and is situated through the village of Kako Petros. It would take a two-hour drive from our villa to the gorge. The narrow roads were quite good despite being high up now on the mountain roads, although we were still wary of all the dislodged rocks tumbling down from above the road during the winter months, presenting a dangerous problem for the motorists. A series of tiny hamlets nestle in a cosy shelter of green valley's or along the base of the dominant mountain ranges and totally lost in the mists of time; living and working exactly in the same way as their forefathers did.

We see a collection of ancient farming equipment and tractors with some farmers still using mules to pull rickety wooden carts, overloaded with fodder for their goats or sheep. Large areas are planted in straight lines of olive trees and grapevines on meticulously cultivated land, with some ploughed so precariously on steep-sided hills for the hot Mediterranean sunshine to ripen their crops. Any small pieces of land the Greek farmers can cultivate – they will, even risking their lives and farming equipment in doing so. These people are hardworking and remarkably tough men, out in very extreme weather conditions from early morning to late in the evening to make enough money to put food on the table for their families. We have a great deal of love and respect for the Greek people!

Descending down the mountain road we glance across the valley to a huge stone quarry which would be worked by the men hereabouts. An abundance of red poppies line our route with others clustered together in amongst the wild grasses in the fields.

Chris parked the car in the pretty village of Kandanos so we can stretch our legs and take a break. There is yet another war memorial dominating the village square, this time we see at its centre the upturned face of a woman carved in white marble resting on a large horizontal sarcophagus. Each of the three sides of the sarcophagus has a bronze plaque with male and female names on them –

many with the same surnames. Carved on the plaques was the date, 20th May, 1941 The Battle of Crete. We walked slowly around the village and noticed there wasn't many old villas and commercial buildings left, it looked like most of the village was built after the war. We were puzzled by this!

As we reach the far end of the village there is another large stone monument declaring − 'ALL the residents of this village − men, women and children, including babies, were taken out and executed by the German forces in harsh reprisals because the people of Kandanos had killed twenty-five German soldiers, trying to halt their allies landing troops at Suda Bay'

A furious German commander had a large metal notice made stating;

"It was justified to have all the villagers shot in punishment in the village of Kandanos, which would be no more. They will totally wipe out any memory of the village and raise it to the ground"

It left us feeling very sad and deep in thought as we drove away from the village, we could just about see the burnt out remains of some old houses, now totally overgrown and abandoned − a stark reminder of how cruel war can be. At that time, we hear the German soldiers even blew up the graveyard in the village.

Continuing along, the scenery was slowly changing again, reminding us of the beautiful Kirkstone Pass in the Lake District with its wild, bleak and rugged landscape. Wild heather grows in abundance on the peaty moorland surrounded by many large rocks left over from the Ice Age. I did wonder if they have the equivalent of moorland grouse here like they do in England. The temperature had dropped very sharply now, I think it must be as cold here as in England in the wintertime with their snowfall and cold winds, we had finally reached the summit of the Lefka Ori Mountains.

Our first glimpse of the sea eventually came into view as we began to rapidly descend downhill until we reached the village of Kalamos nestling in the very toes of the mighty Lefka Ori. The pretty church in the village was large and impressive, dominating the square along with a cluster of shabby houses, unkempt and in a poor condition; a sharp contrast to their magnificent place of worship.

With an impressive tree-lined avenue of mature plane trees greeting us on our approach, planted in two arrow-straight rows like watchful sentinels, their graceful branches arcing over to form a leafy green tunnel whilst cascading down to sway gently to and fro in the warm breezes. The constant impressive peeling on their creamy multi-coloured bark reminded us of the shedding skin of a snake.

Soon we arrived at the pretty seaside resort of Paleochora to park and walk for a while and enjoy the afternoon sunshine. The neatly paved walkway dominates the centre of the town and runs parallel to the delightful promenade. The promenade is pleasant with the clear blue Libyan Sea lapping gently onto a shingle beach. Lined with many tempting restaurants and tavernas we spent a couple of hours walking around and enjoying the sunshine and seashore.

Relaxing by the sea, we watched two old fishermen mending their nets on the quayside as we ate cooling ice cream to quench our thirst. Another fisherman was busily preparing his little sun-bleached boat in readiness to take out to sea later when the tide was right. My eyes began to close and I turned my face up to the sun and breathed a sigh of contentment, then Chris said, "Have you seen the time?" Shaking myself awake again I peered down at his watch and saw the hands were pointing to 4:00 pm. Collecting our things together Chris said it will take us about three hours to get home around 7:30 pm.

On the way back we laughed and pointed to a very large fat pig grazing contently at the side of the road having escaped from its pen. Usually, it's sheep or goats which graze along the road but today it's 'pig on the road' by way of a change!

On the return journey, we stopped for a while to admire a little whitewashed chapel with the added advantage of a wooden porch just outside the old wooden door where worshippers could sit in the shade and listen to the service being conducted from within. The small graveyard below us was crammed full of many traditional crypts placed side by side with only a narrow walkway in between. The Greek people do not bury their dead below ground because the island of Crete is a solid rock below making it difficult. The tradition is, the family buy a piece of ground in the churchyard and successive relations are laid to rest inside the crypt until there are only bones left or until the next member of the family dies, all the graves have a closed glass panel where loved ones leave a picture of the deceased, along with various personal items belonging to them in life. The graves are well looked after and always have flowers and trinkets decorating the horizontal crypt.

The views as always were breath-taking, we looked out across a verdant valley with a magnificent backdrop of mountain ranges in the distance. A repetitive noise made me turn around to see an old man bending over his nanny goat with his hands moving in a constant rhythm, he was milking her. I realised then that the swishing noise was the steady stream of goat milk being squirted into a large metal bucket.

We continued down the narrow winding roads watching the landscape change again dramatically and spotted a large cluster of wooden beehives placed side by side amongst some whinberry or bilberry fruit trees. Further along, we saw a farm with approximately 13 wind turbines neatly placed along the top of a ridge, their blades turning very fast and steady as the strong warm winds generated power. There seems to be more and more wind turbines on Crete now, and we praise the Cretan people for their mindfulness of natural wind power and solar energy.

We were now entering the fruit growing areas just outside Chania town. So many orange trees, as far as the eye can see on both sides of the road. All the trees were heavy with fruit, their large branches bowed down and covered in large juicy oranges ripening in the Mediterranean sunshine just waiting to be harvested for the local markets. Further along I pointed to another large orchard of ripening fruit, this time the trees were full of plums and apricots. The well-tended orchards stretched for about three or four miles down each side of the road, the plantations stretching as far back as the eye could see with some butted up to a rock face giving shelter from the harsh winds in the wintertime.

We drove through the sleepy villages of Karanou and Hilariou with many more orange groves parallel to the road. A few oranges had fallen off the trees and were rotting by their base. We were now coming into the vine-growing area with their short stubby growth, giving maximum strength to the vine and the forthcoming bunches of grapes.

Leaving behind the pretty villages nestling in the mountains of The Lefka Ori, the clean golden beaches and the crystal blue sea, the large expanses of fruit orchards and the tiny white churches overlooking verdant gorges. The clear water of snowmelt as it tumbles down over rocks and boulders worn smooth by hundreds of years pounding and reshaping the landscape. We returned home after another long and exciting day out. Tired and happy to sit out under the stars eating supper and discussing the day's events, and look forward to another adventure sometime soon!

Coastal Resort of Agios Pavlos

June

We said goodbye to the beautiful Cretan springtime and *'yassas'* to a Mediterranean summer. With the arrival of summer, our routine changed dramatically, rising very early to get all our physical jobs done in and around the villa to planning our sightseeing and walking expeditions in the mountains along with cool coastal resorts. On the first day of June, we decided to drive down to the South of the island and spend a full day at the delightful seaside resort of Agios Pavlos.

Up and out early again, we made our first coffee break in the bustling village of Spili, and chose a pretty taverna with a shaded veranda in the middle of the central square, adjacent to the 13 lion heads spewing mountain water from their mouths. We thought we would avoid going to our friend George's taverna today because we are usually there for at least two hours enjoying his hospitality.

Whilst watching the world go by and drinking coffee, a large battered van drove past and packed to the gills with old boiler hens in cages stopping outside the taverna as the driver called out his prices in loud monotone through a big tannoy. We watched in amusement as a few old guys who had been playing *tavli* (backgammon) sauntered over to take a look at the scrawny hens, a few words were exchanged then one guy waving his hand in the air and shaking his head he loudly declared, "The hens were old and no good." Before the disappointed farmer could get in his van and drive away, the coach driver coming the opposite way started shouting at him angrily and said 'he was blocking the road'. He was actually, as the hen man had parked his van on the narrowest part of the main road, and as other vehicles backed up behind him along with the coach, all hell broke loose with lots of car horns coupled with angry shouting. We started laughing, because it looked for all the world like some comedy farce, needless to say, the hapless 'hen man' got in his van and drove away as quickly as possible.

Driving through the winding roads with the car windows open, we see many fields of tall grasses gently swaying and rippling like waves rushing onto the beach. With the constant hot summer sunshine to dry the fields, they can get a good harvest for animal feed and bedding later in the year. The large impressive hills rise up out of the valleys, nestling below us are several small hamlets.

Austere grey stone and slate with occasional flashes of limestone outcrop become evident on the steep hillsides as we journey along. Large potholes in the road caused Chris to swerve around them and avoid an accident or damage to the car. Occasionally, we see evidence of heath fires caused by the constant searing heat from the previous summer, scorched heath and blackened trees surround us giving the landscape an eerie feeling as we continue along the road.

The gorge valley widened now, giving us a magnificent view of the Libyan Sea along with the austere upper edges of the large undulating hills. Bereft of any plantation whatsoever, it's just a mass of jagged grey granite rocks rising in a series of severe peaks. We were now approaching the sleepy hamlet of Saktoria, built centuries ago on a jutting ledge in the hillside and hanging over a deep verdant gorge. Chris slowed the car down, and we looked across to the little village suspended over the gorge with magnificent views, you could live there quite happily as a hermit, an artist, or a writer and chill out completely from the outside world, such beautiful views would inspire anyone. Lovely today when the sun is shining and soft breezes are blowing in from the sea, but come the winter months with heavy rain and strong winds, it would be a different matter.

We began descending the corkscrew road, looking at the little coves and inlets dotted along the rugged coastline of Agios Pavlos. The crystalline water lapped onto a fine sandy beach, many local families and tourists are relaxing or swimming in the clear shallows, with some having lunch under a shady pagoda. The fertile alluvial plain slopes down to meet the sea, with local vegetable crops, vines and olive groves in healthy abundance providing food and a regular income for the local people. The sparkling blue sea is as calm as a millpond, shimmering like jewels in the hot afternoon sun, making it difficult to see where the horizon ends and the blue sky begins. We approach a tiny single-track road, on either side, there are huge flowering geraniums, their heads a blood red and as big as dinner plates.

Parking the car on the marina overlooking the sea, our legs were stiff from sitting in the car for a long time, we longed for a cool drink in the shade before deciding what we would like to do first during the afternoon. We found a table with a lovely view of the beach and sea, the warm breezes caressed our nut-brown bodies, wearing only cotton shorts and tee-shirts we ordered our drinks. Sipping some freshly squeezed orange juice, our eyes travelled over the bay and up towards a series of craggy cliffs lining the far end of the headland. Chris pointed up towards a narrow footpath leading away to the top of the cliffs and suggested we put our boots on and see where the path goes.

Walking down to the beach sometime later and onto the fine sandy beach we stopped to watch a local man bent over, collecting something from the rock pools then placed them in a large canvas bag which he slung over his shoulder, we think they were probably sea urchins as it is one of the local delicacies in Crete. Following the sandy path, we see a young father holding his child's hand paddling in the shallows and watching shoals of tiny fish darting over their feet, bright sunlight caught their silver scales producing bright sparks of light in the water as the young child squealed with delight!

Climbing over a few large rocks almost black in part and covered in algae, we found a delightfully secluded cove and decided to have our picnic there later in the day. Climbing up the steep narrow pathway with an old rickety wooden handrail to stop people from toppling over the side of the cliff face, we paused to catch our breath and admire the magnificent panoramic views over the bay, in the far distance the hills and mountains of the Psiloritis.

The footpath took us over to the very edge of the cliff, we could see a series of massive rocks rising up out of the sea far below us. Over a long period of time along with the constant pounding sea, a large hole in the rocks had been etched out to make an impressive 'picture frame' of the beautiful sea and sky. Walking along the narrow dusty path we move away from the edge of the cliff to meander through some carelessly strewn rocks and boulders at a time when the tectonic plates collided many years ago, and remain there untouched ever since. Their impressive markings ranged from sandstone and slate blue to burgundy and vivid reds, hidden amongst them grow many thorny sea-loving shrubs and hardy rock plants their vivid splashes of deep reds and purple; they are safely sheltered beneath the rocks.

Eventually, we reached the other side of the bay with a few other secluded beaches, some only big enough to accommodate a courting couple or a topless sunbather wishing to be private. The circular walk brought us back down to the top end of the village and back to our car to get the picnic.

We returned to the little cove we had discovered earlier, pleased that no one else had claimed it, we laid the beach towels down and opened up the picnic. Sitting beneath a natural overhang, it had a magnificent stripy coloured rock face, in some parts of the cliffside there was deep burgundy splashes etched into them. It was cool and shaded there, a good ten degrees cooler as we settled down to eat our appetising picnic lunch with a flask of chilled water. I tried to concentrate on reading my book but my eyes were drawn to watching families enjoying themselves in the sea, distracted, I began collecting some small burgundy stones which had come loose from the rocks, to take home with me to make my mosaic pictures on canvas.

A little while later, I pulled off my boots and socks and carefully climbed over the small rocks to have a paddle and look for fish and crabs. Flicking my feet up and down in the clear water, I could see right down to the bottom and lazily watched lots of tiny fish darting over my stilled feet. I began relaxing again, gazing through half-closed eyes and daydreamed for a while in the sun's delicious warmth. After a while, Chris joined me and we watched a large starfish for a while clinging to a green alga covered rock and partially under the water. I pointed to another one, which was just visible and curled around a stone, so lovely and perfectly formed. We began to look closer now, and spotted even more tiny fish, along with a sea spider and some small crabs hidden beneath the rocks.

We could have stayed on our polished rocks forever, daydreaming in the dappled sunshine and partial shade as the afternoon sea breeze cooled our sunburnt arms and legs, happy to watch families playing with their children. With a gentle hum of a bee or a distant twitter of a migrated bird occasionally breaking through the happy laughter. Our gaze drifting down once again to observe the silvery fish darting around the rock pools along with the reclusive starfish – "Ahhhh! This is heaven!" I whispered to Chris, closing my eyes and tilting my face up to the sun's rays again.

But! It was getting late and we needed to set off home again, returning to the car we saw a toddler and her daddy paddling in the shallows, every time she bent down to pick a little stone up and throw it back into the sea her chunky nappy would dip down and come up wet through!

Unfortunately, we had to climb back into the car, by then it was like an overheated oven, but our wonderful day at Agios Pavlos made it all worthwhile.

Chapter Thirteen
Kallergi Refuge Above the
Ormalos Plateau

There is just one small settlement on the plateau, it's Ormalos – and situated in the heart of the plateau. There is a regular procession of cars and coaches driving along the main highway, on their way to visit and walk the famous Samaria Gorge. Few people live here all year round when the winter months are harsh with copious amounts of snow and heavy rain, when springtime arrives the land is usually waterlogged with small lakes here and there. During the summer months many farmers and families move back to the plateau to tend their goats and sheep or cultivate their land with cereals and potatoes.

Today, we will be doing the steady climb up the dusty winding track leading to the Kallergi Refuge, where we can look down onto the beautiful Samaria Gorge below us and maybe see some birds of prey that nest in the gorge face.

I made a vegetable quiche and apple pie the previous day to take with us and share the picnic with our two friends who live nearby. Waking at 7:00 am with the promise of a lovely day we packed the rucksack with everything we were likely to need, hats, sun cream, mosquito bite cream, BOOTS, MAP AND COMPASS. A quick bite of breakfast washed down with a hastily drunk coffee we knocked on our friend's door to say we were ready to go.

Heading in the general direction of Chania on the National Road just after 9:00 am the air was still cool and comfortable inside the car. I had the map to navigate the way, we needed to turn off the main road shortly before Chania and follow the plateau sign to reach the village of Ormalos.

The rich fertile land rustled with wheat and barley; the gentle breezes rippled over the ripening tops like a lovely golden sea. There were also the occasional 'breaks' in the sea of grain with delicate patches of blood-red poppies nodding their heads as we passed by. Large flocks of sheep grazed in the distance, cropping the lush succulent grasses freshly grown from the heavy rain and snowmelt during the wintertime. There was very little snow left on the Psilortis now it is June. We continued driving through a few more sleepy villages and tiny hamlets for a little while.

We eventually reached our destination, parking at the bottom of the hillside to climb up to the Kalergi Refuge Hut. Putting our walking boots on with hats and sunglasses to avoid the glare we started the slow climb to the top. The walk covers nine kilometres on a stony track with sparse shelter from the increasingly hot sun, so we slathered ourselves with high factor sun cream and covered the back of our necks with a scarf then pulled our hats low over our eyes. The Refuge is 1,677 metres above sea level, it is a steady journey to the top but the rewards will be great.

Ten minutes into our walk we saw a large ornate building adjacent to the path and decided to take a look. It was a partially built hotel now abandoned, the once impressive door was hanging on its rusting hinges. We stood in the main reception room which had become a shelter for the goats, the beautiful tiled floor almost covered in their droppings. In one corner were an impressively large stone fireplace and the remains of a small fire someone had recently lit. Over to the far side was the reception desk built in a rich warm mahogany wood, but over time it had become warped and stained with neglect.

Wandering around from room to room we saw more damage done by locals, all the wall lights had been ripped off the walls and the 'white goods' in the restrooms had been stolen. We climbed up the stone stairs to the top floor and saw a few windows had been smashed and broken off their hinges, encouraging wild birds to make their home inside the rooms. Leaving the once lovely but derelict hotel behind, we talked about what may have happened to stop the completion of the hotel. "Maybe they ran out of money during the recent austerity measures. It's so sad to see a lovely building like that fall into disrepair."

The narrow stone path wound around the mountainside, and we climbed higher and higher to reach the low drifting clouds. "Wow," I remarked, pausing for a while and looking over to the splendid views, as far as the eye could see. "Now I have my head in the clouds," I said laughing. "So, what's new Patti," Chris replied.

We met a young Greek couple with their mother on the path, they were resting in the shade under an overhang of rocks and drinking water. We stopped to talk to them for a while and rest, talking to them about the walk. They said they were from Athens on a two-week holiday with their mother, adding they were just about to take her back down again as she was tired. We said our goodbyes and continued up again, the loose stones were digging into our boots making it hard going, along with the boiling hot sun reaching midday now. After a few more water stops we eventually reached our destination and Kalergi Refuge. It had taken us two hours hard slog, but the rewards would be wonderful.

It was hard going but well worth the effort, as we turned to see the manager of the Hut coming out of the building. He asked us what we would like to drink as we made ourselves comfortable in the cool shade of the terrace. Our attention was drawn to a party of eight German walkers on the next table busily pouring over a large map of the area. They all spoke in loud voices, wildly gesticulating and trying to shout louder than the other to get their point of view across. We relaxed in the cool shade of the terrace for a while, sipping our refreshing drinks and talking about the walk up to the Refuge.

My attention turned to the Refuge itself, a modern stone building, elegantly styled with many large windows to let in maximum light. Through one of the open windows, the refectory had six or seven large trestle tables with many chairs running down its length over the lovely polished wooden floor. A few walkers who were staying overnight were still chatting over their lunch. I decided to take a quick look inside the doorway leading into the refectory and saw a large rack of rubberised sandals which you were expected to wear before entering the rooms.

Returning to the shade of the terrace again, I leant back and closed my eyes; the vociferous party of walkers had gone and silence had returned. A cooling breeze blew across the plateau, and I looked out towards the magnificent mountain ranges, the topmost peaks were almost eye level with us, gracefully sweeping down to meet the very beautiful Samaria Gorge far below. First to make a move were our friends who had jumped up, totally refreshed and walked over to the far side by the stone wall running along the outer perimeter of the plateau. We caught their drifts of admiration as they hung over the wall admiring the views far below them. Chris and I were very comfortable, enjoying our second drink when they shouted over to us to come and take a look. "It's one of the most stunning views I have ever seen." I pointed to a large bird of prey slowly circling on the warm thermals, almost eye level and quite near to us. Nearby, there were many massive pine trees and thorny scrub clinging to the walls of the slate-coloured mountains, their deep clefts a home for small clusters of wild olive and deciduous trees in this wild and wonderful place.

We tentatively peered over the stone wall to the sheer drop below us and watched some walkers in the Samaria Gorge slowly advancing in a single line like a colony of marching ants. I suddenly stood back when my head started spinning, and the ground felt like it was shifting beneath my feet, "OH…! I think I'll go back to our table," I said. The stunning views had overwhelmed us all, we became quiet and still and daydreamed – taking in all the wild beauty that is Kalergi.

One of the girls broke the silence with "Oh, I need the toilet".

"Oh, well, that's it then," Chris replied,

"We'd better find a toilet before we start walking back down." I asked Daniel the manager, who was lazily reclining on his homemade canvas swing suspended from the terrace, his dark eyes narrowed against the glare of the sun watching and waiting for more customers. He said we couldn't use the toilets inside the Hut and pointed over to a small wooden shack next to the footpath which is the public toilet. We thanked him and gathered our things together again, setting off back down the mountainside and calling in on the crudely made toilet shed on the way.

Jacqui led the way as she was quite desperate to use the loo by then, she pulled at the rope handle attached to the door and peered in. A loud shriek emitted from her followed by an equally loud "Oh! My Gawd! I can't use this." She moved to one side for the rest of us to look in to see the toilet was suspended out over the Samaria Gorge, 1,677 metres down. We all started laughing and I risked one foot on the uneven rickety wooden floor whilst tightly gripping the rope handle. Nervously taking a peep inside, the homemade toilet had a large pan lid covering the gaping hole with some rough-cut wooden planks for the seat! I gingerly lifted the pan lid and realised to my horror, I was staring straight down into the Gorge itself! It was my turn to shriek loudly and beat a hasty retreat.

"There's no way I could feel safe using that toilet," I said to Jacqui who nodded in agreement but watched Chrissie taking some photographs to show family and friends in England. "They will never believe this if I haven't got proof," Chrissie said, laughing out loud. "No one would believe me if I didn't take some pictures to show them," Chrissie added. Needless to say, none of us used the toilet but found a secluded spot instead to relieve ourselves on the way down the mountain.

"Well, that's one for the book," I said to Chris on the way down again. It was pleasurable walking down as it had turned a little cooler with a fresh wind blowing across the mountainside. We discussed coming back again another time and staying overnight so we could walk from the refuge and higher up into the mountains on one of the many single tracks – well signposted and easy walking.

We were all starving hungry and thirsty again by the time we reached the car, pulling off the walking boots we sat down in the shade to enjoy our picnic. None of us wanted the day to end and we talked endlessly about the fabulous walk and the wonderful things we had seen including the birds of prey. Daniel told us the eagles make their nests in the thick pine trees opposite to the hut, he said he sometimes sees the chicks peeping out of their nests being fed by the adults, and then when they are older, they are encouraged to exercise their wings with their parents in the warm thermals.

Summer Time and the living is easy!

Homelife in the beautiful North West Crete became a very relaxed way of life, with many different experiences when we are out walking, on the beautiful coastline and beaches, the magnificent rugged mountains or walking down the lovely and seldom undiscovered gorges which litter the island. The weather was increasing in its intensity on almost a daily basis and dramatically changing our routine. We were woken early one morning with the melodic sound of migratory birds, coupled with a distant bleating of sheep and goats in the olive groves behind our villa just as it was coming daylight. Sleeping had become difficult, we left the air conditioning on all night in the bedroom, but even on the lowest setting you could hear a constant humming noise, so we kept the shutters closed all day to try and keep the bedroom cool.

My first job of the day was to sweep the patio area around the villa and 'dead head' our massive tree geraniums which have shot up since spring. I have found that the more I do this the longer the plants seem to last, so we enjoy a very colourful display all through the summer and into autumn. Huge dinner plate heads of deep red, pink and white line the patio as I sweep and listen to the bird's morning song. A few years ago, we borrowed a pretty canary from some friends who had a large aviary nearby, we called him 'Super Mario' because he would sing from morning till night. I would put his cage on the low wall outside the patio doors while we were having our breakfast, he loved the sunshine and would sing his heart out. One morning when he was in full chorus, we heard another wild bird singing back to him in our olive trees, and when we looked closer it was another canary of the same colouring, pale cream and brown who was answering our little songster. Mario would sulk when we were getting ready to go out, he would stop singing and turn his back on us and I would end up apologising and telling him "We won't be long."

Chris shouted out of the kitchen window, "Patti your coffee is ready, come and get it."

A tiny brown lizard about six inches long darts out of the way of my sweeping brush and into the thick undergrowth. "The polecats have been again last night and left a few parcels," I retorted as I sipped my coffee. "The lemon-scented geraniums the locals called 'Barbarossa' have masses of mauve flowers on them and it's getting hotter out there."

We sat outside in the cool shade to eat breakfast, enjoying the fresh morning air for a while and reading our walk's book, planning another walk very soon. I tried to read but found it difficult as there were so many distractions. Staring at the tranquillity of the deep blue sky and mesmerising cloud formations, I daydreamed for a while until my neck started aching. The gentle rustling of the olive trees just outside our door has many tiny creatures hidden beneath the thick foliage. It's fascinating to watch different insects and birds which we never see in England, extracting nectar from the flowers or scurrying around nearby. We love to see a 'humming bee' gently hovering over our lemon-coloured roses, one day I managed to get quite near to watch its curling proboscis quickly flicking in and out to extract pollen. Its little wings beating so fast they become a blur as it steadily hovered over the flower heads. On closer inspection, I could see its eyes – two little black dots on a pink coloured face. It had a bulbous rear end with distinctive black and white stripes, I was fascinated! There is another insect some locals call the 'B52 bomber' it's much bigger than an English wasp and a darker colour but it has a terrible sting if you are unlucky enough to get in its way. We get praying mantis and locusts in our garden, we hear the mantis is good for the garden as it will eat aphids and other garden pests, but when the locust gets blown over to Crete from the hot winds of the Sahara – they will strip plants in a day and do a lot of damage to crops. We also get the little geckos which will sneak into the villa when the door is open, there again, they will eat anything edible such as mosquitos and other flying insects. I like to see them on the walls of our villa because they look cute staring down from a safe distance. There is also a Baltic Lizard – quite harmless and they will eat small bugs and insects, it's the mosquitos which are the worst creatures, they have bitten us both quite badly over the years. After trying different methods of relief, we have found that taking B1 vitamins, once a day for a few weeks before flying out abroad helps enormously, they still bite you but apparently, you don't taste nice, it changes the taste of your blood, so they retract quickly.

It was getting increasingly hotter by the day and I felt sure I was slowly melting, the thermostat by the door, read 150 degrees Fahrenheit! We needed a day out, and what better than to go to one of the beautiful beaches we have found. We chose Triapetra in the Southern part of the island where we hoped it would be cooler and more comfortable. Packing our beach things the night before, we took some frozen water in the cool box and set off very early before the sun got too hot. We saw our old friend 'Yeorgi' standing outside his taverna in Spili as we sailed past, a few old guys were sitting outside drinking their morning coffee and putting the world to rights. A glance at one old man got me wishing I had the talent to sketch his face, he had so many deep lines and wrinkles etched in the brown leathery skin. His brown eyes twinkled, turning to slits as he laughed at a comment one of his companions had made. Some other old men were sitting in the shade nearby, their large droopy moustaches popular with the Cretan Mountain men, along with thick wiry beards and course grey hair.

Heading in a similar direction as Agios Pavlos for a while, we turn off further down the coast and opened all the car windows to let the cooling breezes come in as we sped along. Eventually, the deep aquamarine sea came into view with the contrasting grey mountains rising up to our left as we began to descend down the winding road to the beach. With a narrow bumpy stone track running parallel to the edge of the shingle beach we followed the road up to its end. A few villas were perched on the edge of the road with splendid views looking out at the Libyan Sea. The strong hot winds almost whipped the car door from my hand as we climbed out to stare at the view this was soon followed by an even strong gust, almost blowing us off our feet, we clung tightly to each other to avoid being blown off the road and into the sea. "Wow! You could dry your washing up here in less than an hour."

We drove back along the coast road and parked the car under a large shady tree, collecting our beach bag filled with towels, books and sun cream. Walking down the wooden decking which overlaid the fine shingle beach, we headed towards a cluster of brightly coloured umbrella's sheltering the sun loungers and facing the sea. The hot winds blew stronger and stronger, as we sat reading it started kicking up a lot of dust and fine stones which peppered our arms and legs with such sheer force. Trying to ignore the discomfort for a while we gave up and decided to walk over to the taverna on the beach opposite and get a drink. Holding my hat down to stop it from blowing off I carried the beach bag to try and get respite from the increasingly strong winds. Some prettily decorated tables overlooking the beach and sea were placed on a neatly manicured lawn and out of the wind. Across the path were some more sun loungers and open umbrellas on a smaller lawn, partially enclosed by some mature trees. Chris ordered a light lunch for us from a delightful young man and later we took our complimentary raki and sweet almond cake across to a little table attached to the base of a large parasol and made ourselves comfortable for the remaining afternoon. We watched more and more sunbathers disappear from the water's edge to find a sheltered spot like us as the wind continued to blast the remaining hardy few with shingle and dust. We know there are many strong winds like this blowing across from Libya to the South of Crete, so strong it blows the water out from resident's swimming pools. We are fortunate where we live in the Northern part of the island, we still get the hot winds blowing up a storm but not as bad as in the South.

After breakfast, one fine sunny morning, we decided to go and explore the pretty village of Agia Paraskevi (Saint Friday) we needed to drive a short way down the hillside from our home and park in Adele village, then walk a few kilometres through the narrow winding roads, passing olive groves and farms on the way. Agia Paraskevi is a lovely traditional village set back in the hillside and overlooking the sea. It still retains a lot of old-world charm, with a nice mixture of new properties on the outskirts of the village, and a hotchpotch of old villas running along its centre. The narrow winding streets curve gently round, so narrow in part that only pedestrians can walk. A very beautiful church dominates the square at the far end of the village and the street narrows dramatically, making a cul-de-sac at its end.

We entered the church through an impressive wooden door to see an elderly lady busily cleaning and mopping the beautiful tiled mosaic floor. A double-headed eagle in black mosaic was suspended over the far end of the interior. Many colourful icons were displayed down each side of the pristine whitewashed walls with an ornate gold leaf chandelier hanging above our heads. The lady greeted us, pulling out two chairs for us to sit for a while in the quiet coolness of the church. The hot morning sun had been left outside the thick wooden door, the thick creamy stone walls of the church repelled the heat of the day, giving us time to enjoy the quiet peace and solitude; to sit and meditate for a while and recover from the steep hill climb.

Walking around the village, we were greeted by one or two local people who wished us *Kali Mera* (Good Morning). We spotted a small wooden sign leading up to another little church on the outskirts of the village and decided to see where it went. Passing a chicken pen on one side of the path with a lush green overgrowth on the other, we came to a whitewashed church almost hidden away from view behind some mature leafy trees. Walking over a little packhorse bridge with an arid riverbed running into the church courtyard itself, we descended some worn stone steps. To the right of the concrete courtyard was some stone terracing, purposefully built for worshippers to come and sit outside and listen to the service. As the bleached wooden door was ajar, we knocked softly and peeped around to see a young man bending down doing something to a section of wooden panelling.

"*Yasso* (Hello)!" I called, he turned around and beckoned us to come in. Introducing himself he told us that he had been commissioned to restore the church to its former glory and told us that all the wood inside the church was infested with termites. "They have eaten away parts of a large wooden icon of great importance and there is an infestation in the iconostasis, the large wooden screen between the nave and the church alter." This depicts the 'Last Supper' of Christ and the Disciples, sometimes with painted scenes of Saints or scenes leading up to the Crucifixion of Christ. Pausing for a while, he told us he was from the Greek mainland and didn't know anyone because he works alone. He said he was a fully trained professional man who has his certificates in all aspects of restoration and his wife is a professional photographer. We talked to him for a while until the young priest of the parish entered and wished us a good day. As the priest had limited English our new friend translated our conversations, added his own thoughts and opinions about various topics. I asked the priest how the name Agia Paraskevi came about. "It is the Saint who heals eyes and eyesight," he said. He showed us a picture of her holding an oval bowl with a large pair of eyes staring back at us. Then he waved us over to a small tap in the wall by the iconostasis, kneeling down and turning the tap on; he held both hands under the water as it ran down into a small carved stone trough underneath. He pressed his fingers to his eyes for a moment then slowly got up and explained that this is Holy Water to heal bad eyes and eyesight and motioned for us to copy him which I did!

Oh, my poor knees on this hard floor, I thought as I bathed my eyes in the cool spring water. *I wonder if they have a Saint for bad knees.* The priest went on to say that on July 25 and 26, there will be a gathering of people from the village and outlying area for a church service to celebrate Saint Friday's Day. He asked us if we would like to come and join them, we said we would try to. It was now time to leave the restorer to get on with his work but not before I asked the priest what he thought of lady ministers being ordained in England. He thought for a moment and pointed to the old curved stone step, worn smooth and misshapen through centuries of use. Looking at us, very seriously, he said, "No, women are supposed to tread on this step or enter into the Holy Altar as it brings the temptation to men like Adam and Eve." Shaking hands with them both, we thanked them for their time and friendship with the promise we would come again for the celebration of Agia Paraskevi in July.

It was a lot easier walking back downhill to where we parked the car in Adele and still only mid-afternoon, so we decided to go and explore the Old Town. Crossing the road and entering down one of the narrow high sided alleyways we come across the haphazard jumble of many single-storey villas having been built at right angles along a continuous rabbit warren of dusty narrow streets and giving cool shade from the hot sun. Passing the little church in the village square it chimed loudly making me jump and noticing the structure had been built in a warm sandstone familiar to this part of Crete. Cut into large square blocks with an ornately carved stone tower revealing two cast iron bells and a thick sisal rope attached. The weather-beaten doors were locked against us so we stood on tiptoe to peep in through the small dusty windows as our eyes caught the huge brass chandelier hanging from the high ceiling. The beautiful golden cross was centrally placed on top of a white lace altar cover. To each side of the cross were two elegant candlesticks, again in a bright golden colour, whether they were brass or gold I could not tell.

We continued our exploring and came across a quaint little shop and the living quarters of someone's home with an open courtyard displaying many home-spun textiles. Inside there were many pieces of ancient bric a brac from days long ago, old kitchen pottery and cast-iron pans were attractively displayed along the courtyard walls as well as some ancient farming machinery. Wooden hand tools lay on the dusty cobbled floor as we stepped inside from the heat of the day to the comparative coolness of a traditional Cretan home. I rubbed my eyes for a moment adjusting them to the gloom of the old stone interior as my eyes fell on a plump elderly lady sitting huddled over her knitting. She was dressed in black in the old traditional Cretan way, her hair and neck were covered in a tight black scarf which finished low over her forehead, she wore a long-sleeved black jacket to cover her arms complete with a heavy black skirt which fell to her ankles revealing some black 'sensible' shoes. Her lovely face changed from total concentration on the intricate knitting to a beatific smile, her eyes twinkled in a warm welcome. Soon afterwards an attractive young woman appeared and spoke in her native language with occasional bits of English she remembered from school. She leads us to a large wooden loom that dominated the far corner of the room, climbing onto the seat she begins to work the loom as we watched, fascinated. The wooden shuttle flew back and forth as her busy hands worked in equal time. Pausing for a moment she told us this is a cotton thread on this particular large piece of work, although as the pattern of colour slowly emerges her nimble fingers introduced some contrasting-coloured silk thread into the cloth. She left the loom after five minutes and shows us all the cloths, doilies and table mats she has already made on the loom, along with some thick woollen carpets and rugs she has woven recently. Large bags of brightly coloured wool lie propped up against the stone wall and she tells us that they will be used to make some more carpet and rug designs later.

They were all very beautiful, she pointed out more things she had made whilst I asked her for the prices. Eventually, I chose a beautiful handmade table cloth for a fraction of the price we would buy in England. As she ushered us back to a seat near her mother, she told us both looms belonged to her mother and that she had learnt everything from her as was customary.

We thanked her for their hospitality and she asked us if we would like to stay and have coffee with her and her mother. Sitting on the benches next to the sweet old lady who squeezed my hand and chuckled for a moment in delight. She didn't speak a word of English so it allowed me to try and talk to her in my stilted Greek. Chris took some lovely photographs of us together next to an old wooden dresser which held many old photographs of the family. I told her who we were and where we lived, about our family in England and our grandchildren. She was delighted to hear our news as Angelica, her daughter, returned with the coffee and biscuits to join us in our Greek/English chit chat.

Now, it was time to say goodbye with the promise of coming again soon and look at the lovely things Angelica had made on her mother's old weaving loom.

Chapter Fourteen
Chania – A Large and Beautiful Town

"Let's go to Chania for the day, do some shopping and have lunch," I suggested to Chris the previous evening. "We need some groceries and we can find a pretty restaurant in the Old Town," I added. So early next morning after breakfast we drove out onto the National Road heading towards Chania on the North West Coast where it would take us just over an hour to reach the centre.

Many years ago, Chania was the capital city of Crete, but for some reason, it was decommissioned and the honour has now been given to the even larger bustling city of Heraklion. Both places have modern and busy airports and fly to many places around the globe making Crete a rich, cultured and profitable island.

A happy combination of old and new exists in Chania, the Old Town is where you find a lot of ancient Venetian buildings and architecture – its mysterious, narrow winding streets and high sided buildings have similar structures to their 200-year occupation by the Turks, sheltering locals from the hot Mediterranean sun and bringing welcome comfort inside their homes. Many colourful street sellers call out to come and buy their wares, their voices echoing through the narrow rabbit warren of alleyways. You cannot help but notice the varying influences the Turks, Venetians and Romans introduced, leaving their distinctive mark as well as the melodic strains of Cretan music with underlying exotic Eastern sounds reminding you of some exotic far away Kasbah. The beautiful island of Crete is an archaeologist botanist and geologists dream come true with many archaeological sites discovered and still more to later uncover.

Chania is situated on a Minoan settlement once called Kidonia, still with open sites in the Old Town showing how the Minoans lived and worked with certain areas being inhabited as long ago as the Neolithic period. The Chania of today sprawls out towards the picturesque bay where many cargoes, ferry, passenger ships and liners dock, bringing visitors from all over the world. The

White Mountains rise up to 2,453 metres (three metres short of the Psiloritis, Mount Pahnes has the title of the loftiest peak) in the distance and framing the city, a moving picture of different colours and textures swirl and drift around the mountain range, changing mood with the passing of the seasons. In the hot summer months, the mountains shimmer with blue heat haze and look translucent, in the winter when the snow covers the high peaks its's like a crystalline dusting of icing sugar, glinting and sparkling in the winter sunlight. With the peaks being so high, the freezing cold ice and snow do not melt until the middle of June, when the snowmelt turns into many gushing rivers down the mountainside; pouring into the rivers, gorges and reservoirs. The crystal-clear mountain water is so pure and in some parts of the island where we live in the North West, you can drink the water straight from the tap inside the home, it is quite delicious, clean and healthy without any added chemicals. Unfortunately, the East side of Crete, Heraklion, Agios Nicholias etc. have a borehole instead of mountain water, so they cannot drink straight from the tap and have to drink bottled water instead.

"It's busier than Rethymnon," I remarked as Chris carefully negotiated the car through the main street, weaving in and out of parked cars and abandoned vehicles that had double-parked whilst the owner nipped into a shop for a moment. Motorbikes came up close behind us, riding either side of the cars then suddenly swerve in front without warning. You have got to have eyes in the back of your head, I thought as a 'twist and go' bike surged past us with Dad at the front, Mum clinging on behind and holding a young child in the middle of them, their bags of shopping wedged in around their feet. I am always relieved when we turn off the main road and reach the underground parking area beneath a shopping mall.

We both like Chania as much as the Cretan people do, because it has everything to offer from a wide range of excellent clothing and food shops to classy restaurants and tavernas. The older part of the town has many pretty gift shops selling a wide range of leather goods, clothing, household items and soft furnishings along the alleyways. I remember when we were walking past a tiny local taverna situated down a back street a few years ago and listening to some live music coming from within, we looked in through the open door to see the owner and his wife with another couple. "Come in, come in," the man called to us and beckoned us to some seats. We ordered a drink and he brought us delicious *mezethes*. "On the house!" he exclaimed grinning. The music got louder and so did the two couples, the next moment we are pulled to our feet and encouraged to dance around the tiny floor to the strains of Russian music, the man told us he was Cretan and his wife was from Russia and so were their friends. We stayed for over an hour or so, dancing, talking and laughing with them – it was totally on the spur of the moment, unexpected and so nice but very typical of Cretan hospitality.

Heading towards the pretty harbour and marina, we watched some of the fishermen and yachting fraternity repairing their boats and nets with others sitting in the morning sunshine drinking wine or eating lunch just inside the boats. We love to stroll along the cobbled walkways where so many pretty Cretan restaurants line the route. There is a wide variety of fresh and delicious home-cooked food on offer, their speciality is locally caught fish prepared the same day and served to you al fresco on pretty decorated tables under colourful shady canopies. Another pleasing sight in the summer months is the open-topped landaus taking tourists along the cobbled promenade and through the old town which runs adjacent to the Venetian City Walls. All the horses are well-groomed and cared for, their beautiful manes and tails are often plaited with pretty coloured ribbons whilst their leather bridles and harnesses are highly polished along with the decorated horse brasses.

We aimed to walk to the furthest point of the marina and passed by the Venetian shipyard building erected in 1599, its magnificent open-ended structures facing out towards the sea. Originally there were 17 warehouses in number but now only seven remain, they are in the process of being carefully renovated and restored to their original condition with the added interest of a maritime museum now in its construction. The soft gentle breezes caress our sunburnt skin blowing in from the sea, passing by one or two eager restauranteurs trying their best to persuade the tourists to come and eat. Heading inland again towards the shops, weaving in and out of other shoppers and sightseers we stop for a while to admire some beautiful displays of jewels and diamonds twinkling behind the jeweller's windows. Elegant mannequins pose gracefully behind large plate glass windows wearing the latest fashions, designer shoes in soft leather from Italy and Spain along with many unusual styles of handbags to match. There are a few bookshops, beach ware and souvenirs next to expensive children's clothing with tiny shoes. Street sellers are calling out their wares selling hot chestnuts, potatoes or sugared doughnuts. The atmosphere is exciting with our heads turning this way and that, admiring everything wonderful Chania has to offer.

An elderly man and woman obstruct the middle of the pavement in the process of having a very loud argument, the man is clearly winning because he is shouting louder than his wife who appears to be backing down. He waves his fist at her and screams abuse quite oblivious to other people passing by. A small queue is forming behind us as we try to shuffle past them along the now narrow pavement. I tried hard not to stare incredulously at this elderly man abusing his wife but it was hard not to. Eventually, we reached the other side of the pavement and I looked back at the people who were following on behind me, no shock or amazement registered on their faces, maybe because they are a nation of hot heads having a row in a public place is not out of the ordinary.

A heady mixture of cooking smells drifts out of another doorway and mingled with the warm afternoon air, with my mouth watering we follow the delicious aroma to the next window. It is a delicatessen, cooked meats, roast chicken and hot pies are attractively displayed on the window bottom along with a large variety of fresh bread and quiches. My stomach made the loudest rumble and we chose a restaurant facing out towards the marina out of the hot sun. We ordered a cool drink and a large seafood platter. On the large platter was a large locally caught sea bass on a bed of creamy mash potato its mouth slightly ajar with its glassy eyes staring up at us, this was surrounded by pink prawns, crayfish and lobster claws, there were chunks of salmon and shark meat and mussels on top of crisp green salad leaves, tomatoes and cucumber with green and black olives completing the culinary artwork. Silence reigned for over an hour as we ate at leisure our delightful meal, pausing for a while to drink in such a beautiful setting the sea lapping gently onto the shoreline along with a few gulls calling out in the distance.

Circular Walk from the Seaside Town of Plakias on the South Coast

Mid-June

The seaside resort of Plakias, 35 kilometres from Rethymnon, nestles in a spectacular bay on the South Coast of Crete looking out over the Libyan Sea and surrounded by beautiful countryside along with rolling hillsides. The road enters

Plakias from the East just behind the beach and heads straight onto the main seafront. A lively and friendly place it has everything to offer the tourists and ardent walkers. We found the tourist information centre who gave us the directions of a route we should take to do a circular walk. Plakias is relatively a new town because in the census of 1961 only six fishermen resided here, but with the advent of tourism, it has become a popular tourist destination.

A clean sandy beach and a harbour are centrally placed along the promenade, although further down the beach it becomes stony and this is where many keen snorkelers come to dive in the crystalline waters amongst the rocks to see lots of marine life. We have also watched a few brave climbers scaling up the high rugged rocks facing the bay, not for the fainthearted I might add! Many taverna's and restaurants line the peaceful seafront for locals and visitors to partake of a meal or cooling drink along the shaded pavements and gaze at the magnificent views across the bay and beyond. Just a short walk inland to the town centre you can find many splendid shops which include a supermarket, butchers and bakers selling home produced meats and freshly made bread and sweet cakes; therefore it is self-sufficient and a popular place for ex-pats to live in retirement.

A beautiful day with a warm breeze cooling us and blowing in from the sparkling aquamarine sea, we began our walk turning up past the local Youth Hostel. We were soon climbing up through the olive groves dotted with a few lemons and orange trees along with some small unripe pomegranates slowly ripening in the afternoon sunshine. The tourist guide told us to follow the riverbed keeping it on our right, soon we could hear a steady flow of rushing water coming from down below us, catching glimpses now and then through the dense green lushness of many trees and vines. We came upon an English couple in their late seventies, early eighties who lived nearby and they told us they had walked these paths many times over the years in the summer and winter months, they needed a bit of help to scramble over some rocks and boulders but this did not stop them from coming to do the walk, it just took a bit longer to complete.

Climbing steadily and helping our newfound friends, we walked together for a while through the leafy shade of very tall reed and bamboo canes with some being as tall as ten feet high, so very thick and strong. The little dirt path forks left and right and our friends tell us that on the left side of the path there is a very old whitewashed church set in the rock face and worth going to see. The old man points over to his right and tells us that the little packhorse bridge dates from Venetian times and is just wide enough to receive a donkey or foot passengers over its length. We said we would walk up to the church first and take a look, we left them sitting in the shade on some smooth stone boulders to rest for a while.

The tiny church is elevated by three or four whitewashed sloping steps as we stooped to enter through the open doorway which must have been only five feet in height. The rickety bleached wooden door was hanging off its hinges and propped at a precarious angle against the inside stone wall. Sparsely furnished and very neglected there were a few damaged icons of one or two Saints, plus the usual box of candles, incense and matches. A large wooden cross lay on its side – still beautiful in its way but now neglected and sadly forgotten. The flagstone floor was dirty and badly needed sweeping and repairing. Unfortunately, as with some other churches we have seen, sheep or goats enter in for shelter and add to the mess. Leaving the sad little church behind and coming out into the bright sunlight we were temporarily blinded for a moment or so.

Our friends were still sat down waiting for us and then told us about the ruined mills ahead and the derelict properties nearby. "Follow the narrow path up the steep incline and when you have viewed the ruined mills, turn sharp right and this will take you along the very top of the gorge and eventually into the village of Mirthios," the old man said. "There are a few paths you can take and they all have lovely scenery." We thanked them both for the useful information and said our goodbyes.

We soon came upon the splendid ruined watermill with a distinctively pointed tower and a sheer drop of around ten metres through a vertical stone-built canal. A propeller and the transmission mechanism used to be at the bottom, still very impressive and very interesting we rested for a while pointing out the things of interest. Climbing even higher now and a little more precarious, we carefully watched where we were placing our booted feet for maximum grip on slippery rocks and uneven paths. I stopped briefly to peer over the edge to see a few old wooden beams still attached to crumbling walls but with the absence of the roof. The walk book tells us "At this point climb down into the stream" but as there was still a lot of fast-flowing water and very deep in parts we declined.

Ignoring instruction, we followed a narrow but passable path and with some careful negotiations, we reached the very top of the gorge to rest and enjoy the fantastic scenery all around us. With the gorge far below us we could look out over the top at a mass of lush greenery then peeping through the dense undergrowth we could just see the mill tower and partial ruins, then further down to the town of Plakias and out over the blue Libyan Sea.

"Wow! What a view."

We climbed a little bit further along the path and towards the end, it got a bit nerve-racking because some of the ground had recently fallen away so we had to take a step across and grip hard onto a rusty metal fence staked into the ground and quite loose. Steeling ourselves, we had to quickly swing around it to a firmer piece of ground, temporarily suspending ourselves in mid-air! If the fence had come away, we would have fallen a great distance to the bottom of the gorge – thankfully we were both okay!

We were now walking on a drivable dirt road and slowly descending towards a cluster of properties built into the hillside which looked out over the vast green vegetation far below. We see a large stone building on our left as we continued to walk parallel with the gorge top. We could hear loud running water and as we approached and saw the first stone reserve tank and above it was a lovely fountain also built of stone containing snowmelt mountain water. Looking inside we admired the beautifully restored building with 17 neatly divided sections where the local women would have come to do their daily washing and collect fresh drinking water for their homes. Each section had a sloping stone where they would have soaped and scrubbed their clothes, with a natural drainage section underneath so the dirty water could run away – Genius! Standing inside under the cool timber beamed roof and out of the hot sun, we could imagine how all the local women would congregate here to do their washing, joke and chat and do some gossiping. My amateur photos didn't do the place justice, on the outside of the impressive building was a lovely restored square with two or three matures trees giving ample shade situated near some neatly carved stone seats to rest awhile. Further down, some more stone fountains and troughs were placed along the outside walls with beautifully carved lion's heads spewing arcs of mountain water, a truly lovely and peaceful place. Chris called me to come and look at a medium-sized freshwater crab sitting at the bottom of one of the troughs and looking up at us, how it had got into the deep stone trough we don't know.

We were slowly walking downhill now and enjoying the sunshine with fabulous views, I point out a few mature bushes growing in great profusion. Many dark velvety purple flowers were covered with lots of large honey bees, their continual humming filled the scented air as they systematically extracted the precious pollen from within the flower heads. "These look like lavender bushes," I called to Chris, he had gone ahead and I had my nose very close to the heady scented flowers. Chris walked back and inhaled the pungent lavender perfume, "It's lavender Patti although I have never seen lavender bushes like this, they must be up to six or seven feet high, very bushy for lavender." We haven't seen this particular plant growing in June/July and couldn't understand why a plant from the lavender family would grow to this height. Everything seems to be bigger in Crete, we have seen Christmas Poinsettias growing like trees, beautiful Mimosa trees with their deep yellow blossom, a variation of heathers, very tall and prolific. In springtime, you see very large bushes of broom and gorse, and don't get me started on the fruit and vegetables – they are truly something else, big, juicy and very tasty, the Mediterranean diet is the best in the world, it's no wonder they live to a ripe old age.

Soon we reached the bottom of the dirt path and walked past the Youth Hostel again and into the town centre, we bought an English newspaper (once a month) to catch up on all the news at home. Sitting in the shade and overlooking the beautiful sea we relaxed with a cold glass of freshly squeezed orange juice.

We watched the sun sink down on the horizon, a fiery arc giving shimmering flames of light against the early evening sky.

Chapter Fifteen
Ancient Aptera

July

One morning after breakfast on the patio, I was busily reading our walking guide in Crete and spotted an interesting chapter about the Ancient Settlement of Aptera. It says it's an impressive settlement 3,480 metres long and was constructed in the fourteenth century, B.C. It suffered from earthquake damage in fourth to seventh century A.D. but with the help of E.U. funding, some remedial work was done on the site to repair and replace the fallen pillars and stonework. We didn't realise how big the site actually was until we began to carefully step over one or two pieces of fallen masonry still waiting to be reinstated to its original structure. To be honest, it isn't what you would call a place of beautifully carved stonework, instead it was an important place of immense interest coupled with a rich and varied history. It would probably have been built by the Romans, and as we walked down the dirt path through the olive groves, we stopped to admire the remains of what once was a magnificent Roman villa overlooking the mountains over to one side, together with lovely clear views of the Bay of Chania. A deep well was in situ nearby with the crumbling remains of a bathhouse, now completely dry it must have supplied not only the impressive villa but many other dwellings nearby. Numerous granite coloured stone pillars had fallen and were now laid on the grass which belonged to the villa. We could imagine how splendid they must have once been, we think there would have been an erected stone pillar every four feet or so along the outer walls of the villa courtyard. It was fascinating to see the precise square, cut into the large and perfectly shaped round base where the fluted upright pillar would have been lowered into place. It always makes me wonder how they managed to erect such large and heavy stonework centuries ago, reminding me of our own beautiful Stonehenge.

A large part of the settlement had been cleared of olive trees and scrubland but there is still much more work to do in the wild olive grove nearby. The remains of a theatre have been found, unfortunately, rough scrub and wild grasses still cover much of the landscape. With some future restoration, the visitor will be able to see how impressive it once was. We came across a prominent stone circle which had been a theatre where players would have acted out a story on an elevated wooden platform, if you look carefully, you can still see the neatly drilled holes running around the arena which fastened the platform in place.

Further along the site, we see a large square sandstone building and our book tells us that this was the Monastery used until 1964 when it was eventually abandoned – why? We do not know, but in other Monasteries, we have visited it meant the last Holy Order of Monks died out. This building was still very beautiful and in good order, well maintained down to growing seasonal plants in large pots in the cobbled courtyard. We look towards the ancient wooden doors leading to the monk's cells where they would sleep or pray in solitude. Centrally placed in the cobbled courtyard was a lovely stone fountain, sadly no longer spewing clean water from its centre. Leading off into one of the small buildings from the courtyard and with the absence of a roof was an arsenal of many large cannonballs still lying in a mounded heap to one side? This comes as no surprise to us, other Monasteries had to fight quite often to protect themselves as well as precious religious artefacts within, some Monasteries even hid allies during the occupation of Crete. Down through the centuries, bandits and pirates would regularly come to raid the lovely old Monasteries and churches stealing gold, silver and precious jewels. We have even seen a few Monasteries abandoned and re-built in a very out of the way place to avoid such as this. Not so far away from this settlement, we came across the remains of two German gun emplacements built during the Battle of Crete to use as a 'look out' over the Bay of Chania.

Finally, a beautiful rose garden with pretty shrubbery had been planted by another building once used as a refectory, a large domed roof and a continuous line of stone seating run down each side of its length, there would also have been an equally large wooden refectory table down the middle of the room to seat all the monks. Returning to the public Roman bathhouse we peered inside and tried to second guess what it must have originally looked like and how busy it must have been. Deals were done, problems sorted out and agreements finalised in many Roman bathhouses.

We had to return to the car and drive further down the site to take a look at the old fortress which had been built on the very edge of a high cliff overlooking the Bay of Chania, an advantageous point to watch for all the enemies looking to attack the island. Unfortunately, there were quite a few different invaders which have successfully done this throughout the centuries! It is a remarkable sight, and we spent a few hours happily browsing around the once important City, built here long before the beautiful city of Chania existed.

The Cretan Food Festival in Rethymnon Town Centre

The yearly Rethymnon Food Festival is in the first two weeks of July, a very significant and entertaining event and held in the leafy central park of Rethymnon. Many local people, farmers, cheesemakers, olive and vineyard growers and tourists come to watch or take part in various amusements and exhibitions starting at 7:00 pm every evening and finishing around midnight.

Now, we were entering the month of July, it was becoming increasingly difficult to venture out anywhere during the scorching daylight hours, let alone plan a walk of any significance. So, our daily routine changed somewhat and we would get up early at daybreak and do our jobs and go shopping before the sun was at its hottest midday. Quite often, we would sit in the coolest place we could find, under a large umbrella on the patio or in the lounge with the air conditioning on. Sometimes resting on the bed for a couple of hours after lunch with the shutters closed until the outside air becomes a little cooler. So, it seemed a jolly good idea when Chris mentioned the Food Festival in the evenings once the sun had gone down and darkness came.

We left the car on the Marina carpark facing the sea and strolled down the wide promenade enjoying the comparative coolness of the early evening. As we drew nearer to the town centre, we fell into step with many Greek families heading the same way as us in a happy state of excitement and anticipation. Some of the children looked cute dressed in their traditional Cretan costumes. Filing in through the large park gates we could hear the familiar sound of happy Greek music coming from within, a wooden platform had been purposefully erected for the two-week event. We stood watching a few older girls and boys from the local school who were dressed in their colourful National costumes, dancing to a lively piece of music. This was followed by a group of little girls and boys their average age was seven years old, they were doing a less complicated dance but well done and nice to watch them perform.

Walking over to a long line of open market stalls that had been set out on each side of the avenues, we enjoyed watching many exhibitions of various types of food and drink. The first stall we approached was piled high with many different local cheeses from the various villages in the mountain regions, they were made with either goat milk or ewe milk and we were invited to taste some of the little squares of cut cheeses on the plates. The next stall had an attractive display of locally produced honey, depending on where the beehives had been placed dictates the kind of honey the bees will produce. There was heather honey from the hills around Rethymnon, sweet honey from the wild and fragrant thyme, we were invited to taste samples from little plastic spoons. Thoroughly enjoying first one and then another I began to feel sick, so in the end, we bought a jar of thyme honey to drizzle on the top of thick Greek yoghurt at breakfast time.

Yet another stall positively groaned under the weight of a delicious selection of homemade biscuits, cakes and a large variety of different shaped bread along with the familiar hard do-nut ring-shaped bread covered with sesame seeds, not recommended, so hard and tasteless it threatens to pull the fillings out of your teeth! Trying to overcome the feelings of nausea after 'pigging out' on samples of honey, I got my second wind and tucked into the free nibbles of cake and biscuits offered to us by a nice lady. It's always interesting when visiting other countries to see what kind of food is produced and sold there, the Cretan food is second to none and the Mediterranean diet is well known for being very healthy.

It was the next stall that made Chris' eyes gleam when we came upon a stall filled with local wines and raki from various regions in Crete. We waited our turn in the queue and watched other people trying shots of red, white and rose wines which had been poured into tiny plastic containers. Eventually, we could take our place at the front of the stall and try one or two samples of red for Chris and a white or rose for me as well as a shot of each of the local raki. We have always found the local village wines in Crete to be very nice, but it was interesting and informative for us to try a more expensive and smoother tasting wine produced in Crete for some of the exclusive hotels and restaurants there.

As we walked away from another stall which held a lovely display of handmade embroidery of table cloths and mats, and beautiful hessian handbags, aprons, napkins and cushion covers with many other tempting items for sale.

Nearby was an old wooden loom with a lovely display of woven rugs draped over its frame, could it be the same one from the village of Adele where we met the mother and daughter.

We headed towards the elevated wooden stage to watch a group of young men who had captivated a large audience and singing some lively songs with many people laughing and clapping to the music and giving lots of encouragement. We found two empty chairs and we sat down to listen to the group. There were five young men, one on the drums, three playing the guitars and a frontman singing in 'broken English' Their clothes were unusual and jazzy and they all had the latest hairstyle of 'messy, controlled' – it suited them and we thought they looked good. As we listened to a very different style of playing and singing, we realised their songs were a 'new take' on some old and familiar-sounding sixties and seventies pop songs. They were really good and we later learnt they all came from Italy. Watching in rapt amusement with a few local kids getting up to do a jive or a twist to the bouncy music, we clapped in time to the beat and sang along with some of the songs we knew.

The evening was still warm and sultry without a breath of wind, a clear night sky hosting millions of bright twinkling stars above us. It was lovely just to sit and relax with only a short-sleeved shirt and jeans on, soaking up the happy atmosphere of everyone laughing, dancing and singing. The hours rolled by quickly and it was midnight when we reluctantly got up and walked slowly back down the promenade and to our car and relating all the lovely things we had seen and done during the evening, Tired and happy we went to bed, looking forward to another new adventure.

Ancient Phalasarna (Falasarna)

It had been our intention to visit the ancient archaeological site of Falasarna this year but other commitments seemed to have got in the way, so we decided to do it sooner rather than later because the sun had become unbearably hot to sit in the car or outside for more than a few hours at a time.

Ancient Phalasarna (Falasarna) is an important Greek harbour town situated on the North West coast of Crete. Built by the Minoans and later 'sacked' by the Romans (evidence of the large stone cisterns) much of the ongoing construction was then erected by the Romans over a period of time, plainly built but totally accurate in their building constructions. The visible remains of the city were built around 333 B.C. and have several imposing sandstone towers and bastions which can still be seen, with a great number of fortifications that once protected the town. The harbour was also enclosed behind the fortified walls giving maximum protection to their boats. The harbour is ringed by stone quays with mooring stones and connected to the sea through two artificial channels. A number of excavations were done in 1986 to reveal many interesting finds of public roads, wells, warehouses, altar and baths. Overlooking the harbour and jutting out into the sea are the remains of a splendid Acropolis, there you will find rock-cut cisterns, wells and watchtowers as well as a splendid temple dedicated to the Goddess Dictynna.

Leaving home as early as possible, we headed in the direction of Chania on the National Road, via the popular seaside resort of Kissamos. Turning inland for a while we followed the 'brown tourist sign' indicating Ancient Phalasarna. Motoring along a secondary road and passing many colourful tourist shops and blousy beach taverna's we began descending the hairpin bends above a narrow coastal plain where farmers have discovered the benefits of plastic greenhouses for forcing tomatoes, melons and cucumbers. Eventually, we reach a small car park facing a beach and park the car well under an overhang of trees to keep the car as cool as possible. Here we must get out and walk along a stony uneven track for one kilometre to visit the large ancient site.

Passing through a small olive grove we came across a large stone 'throne' approximately seven feet high and about four feet wide, this has puzzled experts for centuries as there is no explanation for its function but most visitors including ourselves, sit on the massive construction to have a photograph taken. We were now looking at where the port had once been, and in part, the walls of the inlet. The port was completely dry from the island itself when it had tilted from a powerful earthquake many years ago. As we venture further inland, we see some cut stone which was once part of the quayside, with two or three large blocks having a perfectly shaped large hole where an iron ring would be fastened to tie the boats up inside the harbour. It was hard to believe that all this was once a busy harbour, so high up from the land and away from the sea.

Wandering around for over two hours we discovered some ruins partially enveloped and almost hidden from view, with nature reclaiming the archaeology. Along a narrow path leading toward the sea, we stumbled on a very deep well in front of us, uncovered and without railing or fence around it, it was deep enough for someone to break a leg should they fall into it! Completely dried out now, it would have once served the people residing here in the row of small stone villas on the hillside above us and in an advanced stage of dereliction, but with some imagination, you could see that they must have once been comfortable homes. There had been a recent archaeological dig here as we approached a railed area, revealing several stone walls and partly covered buildings indicating how large and important this City must have been. Further down we came across a large soil pile which must have been the diggings from the site, picking through the soil we saw several calcified seashells from when the sea had totally covered this part of the port.

We went on to look at the impressive rock-cut Roman cisterns where freshwater would have been collected for the city. It was a large feat of stone masonry blocks cut into the rock face itself, we stood at the very edge and looked down into the cool stone depths below. The impressive remains of three massive oblong stone blocks still covering the top of the cistern and are placed horizontally. They looked solid and very heavy and we wondered how the Romans managed to cut and manoeuvre them into place, it was an incredible sight.

Sitting down on some rocks overlooking the sea we enjoyed a cool welcoming breeze blowing in from the startlingly blue sea. Way down below us, we watched a party of six people on a white sailing boat having fun with one or two diving off the boat into the water with some others reclining on the deck sipping wine and nibbling food.

The remains of our bottled water were warm and we had eaten the picnic! Another interesting day had quickly slipped by and we journeyed home again enjoying all the wonderful and interesting things we had seen.

The Historical Museum of Crete

August

Hot and getting hotter. We started getting a bit of 'cabin fever' and decided to drive to Heraklion, the capital of Crete and visit the Historical Museum.

The history of Crete dates to the seventh millennium B.C. preceding the ancient Minoan civilisation by more than four millennia. The Minoan civilisation was the first civilisation in Europe and the first in Europe to build a palace.

When the Minoan empire was wiped out by the Thera eruption, Crete developed into an organised City of states before becoming part of the Roman Empire, Byzantine Empire, the Venetian republic, the Ottoman Empire and then the modern state of Greece. The Historical Museum of Crete in Heraklion was founded by The Society of Cretan Historical Studies in 1953. Many permanent collections highlight the beautiful and varied art and history of Crete from the fourth century A.D. up to and including the second world war. These include ceramics, sculptures, coils and precious gold items, wall paintings and weaving with an accurate reconstruction of a Cretan rural home along with many other beautiful and interesting items to hold any visitors interest on such a hot afternoon.

The ground floor is the place to start and when we walked in through the large wooden doors, we were welcomed by modern air conditioning and a smiling caretaker who asked how old we were. "If you are over 65 years, it is free to come in – if not, it's just ten euros each." At the time we were 63 years old so we paid, and found that it was well worth the money for some interesting entertainment, taking all afternoon to look around the three floors.

The first floor contained sculptures and architectural fragments from the Byzantine, Venetian and Turkish periods. I was immediately drawn to a splendid fifteenth to sixteenth-century tiered fountain from a Venetian palace. Simple but effectively designed, it had two vertical rows of tiny stone cups placed on each side of the fountain and a larger, centrally placed cup at the top. The water then drops from cup to cup cascading down through unseen copper pipes. It is a delightful piece of engineering and I stood admiring it for a long time. There was also some religious art, wall paintings and documents from the Venetian period plus a reconstruction of a domed Cretan church. My interest was drawn to a painting by El Greco, a view of Mount Sinai painted around 1570 and an even smaller piece of work depicting The Baptism of Christ, 1567, only two paintings are held in Crete by the famous artist. There is said to be many more paintings displayed in a museum in Spain even though El Greco was born in Crete.

The upper floor contains a reconstruction of the studies of the writer Nikos Kazantzakis and the Cretan statesman Emanuel Tsouderos with photos and documents relating to the occupation of Crete by the Germans, as well as helmets and parachute harnesses. Further down and beautifully displayed, we see a large selection of local folk art including a wide range of textiles. A recent addition is a re-creation of a Cretan farmhouse complete with a bedroom, living room and kitchen, ancient farm tools and kitchen utensils hold our interest for a while until we go into the café for a drink and rest for a while.

Leaving the air-conditioned museum around 4:00 pm we walked over to one of the taverna's set back a little from the promenade and facing the sea to enjoy a light breeze blowing offshore. We chose a comfortable seat under the taverna's large parasols and ordered a fresh Greek salad along with a large bowl of freshly made chips. Sipping a cooling glass of their delicious local wine we talked about the things we had seen in the museum and remarked how interesting it had all been. The day was cooling down now as we finished our meal and decided to take a stroll through the town and do a bit of sightseeing. We both love the narrow streets and plazas with their lovely atmosphere, sometimes there are street musicians and singers to entertain the public.

The large bustling City of Heraklion is not only the largest administrative capital of Crete but the largest city in all of Greece. The impressive Venetian fortress known as Rocca al Mare was built from 1523–1540 to guard the inner harbour of the city. The original city was founded in 824 A.D. by the Saracens, but in 961 A.D. Imperial forces attacked the city and the Saracens were driven out. The Greek people remained in control and governed the country for a further 243 years when in 1204 A.D. the city was sold to the Venetians. Then in 1664–1669 the Ottoman Empire besieged the city and ruled the island. Between 1898 and 1908 Crete fell under British control until in 1913 the Island of Crete was incorporated into the Kingdom of Greece.

This is a brief resume of the complex history of Crete and its conquerors, one can see how many different influences have left their mark with many beautiful places of worship, music, food and drink. From the commercial buildings, the remarkable Roman architecture and impressive water cisterns to the mosaic floors and exquisite Mosques from the Turkish period.

After our delicious meal, we walked into the Old Town along the lovely narrow streets built in Middle Eastern style, running this way and that with high sided villas and hotels giving coolness and shade to the local people from the harsh sun, strong winds and driving winter rain. The city always has a wonderful feel to it with an air of expectancy and vibrancy. We meandered to the beautifully ornate paved Eletheriou Venizelou Square or simply Lion Square which dates back to the Venetians. Centrally placed in the magnificent square are the most beautiful fountains shooting water high into the air and below are four large stone lions supporting the main bowl. Lending their atmospheric support to the square

are many colourful cafes, restaurants and unusual shops situated in a neat circle set back from the large fountain.

Eletheriou Venizelou was Crete's most famous statesman, he was born and brought up in the mountain village of Theriso, one of the cradles of Cretan independence and the hometown of his mother. The modest house has a plaque commemorating her famous son, he is respected and honoured by the Cretan people. It was here in 1905 the Revolutionary Assembly was held, consequently, we see many street names, parks and gardens proudly displaying his name in memory of a great man.

With so much to see and do in Heraklion, we hear the melodic chimes of a clock in the distance striking 6:00 pm. Our feet were aching and we were tired from all the walking we had done but it was time to leave this interestingly beautiful City and return home. We will come again to do more exploring and discover many more exciting places within the Old City walls.

Chapter Sixteen
Kato Zakros and the Gorge of the Dead

September

After breakfast one morning, Chris found a walk which was on our 'bucket list', but it meant us staying overnight, the place is Kato Zakros and the walk is in The Gorge of the Dead just outside the village and situated at the far east of the island.

The fishing village of Kato Zakros nestles along a pebble and sandy beach with a line of tavernas running along its length. The little harbour is home to a few fishing boats, at the far end are some lovingly restored cottages that are rented out to tourists during the summer months.

There are spectacular views along the clifftop road as we approached the village then the road winds down to join the narrow promenade. We had already phoned ahead to book a room in one of the fisherman's cottages and asked for the keys at the nearby taverna.

The Gorge of the Dead got its colourful name by way of a series of purposefully square-cut rock tombs carved out in Minoan times and even earlier than this. They are set very high on the magnificent gorge walls, when they were first carved out centuries ago. They would have been at ground level but due to earthquakes etc., the island of Crete has tilted over time. The advantage of this is when the winter floods come the fast-flowing river will pass safely beneath them. The walk itself will take two hours (17 kilometres) to do because the path is also in the final stage of the E4 trans-European footpath it is quite well marked once you have left the village.

The Walk:

Follow the signs from the south end of the village opposite the Napoleon taverna for the first half-hour you will walk through some olive groves and smallholdings. The narrow path runs alongside the stream bed marked by the familiar red dot waymarks and occasional signposts. It is a lovely walk and one to do in the springtime when all the wildflowers and herbs are in abundance. As you round a bend in the path and to your left, the gorge spectacularly opens out and you are now looking up at the magnificent rock-cut tombs, pausing for a while to admire the exacting skills from long ago. If you are lucky, you may see some birds of prey circling around high above, exercising their wings and riding on the warm thermals. Eventually, the walk leads you through some banana and olive groves and past The Palace of Zakros.

After a good night sleep in the pretty Fisherman's Cottage, we were up early and heading for the start of the walk to the gorge. The early October sun began peeping through the clouds with the promise of a fine settled day. Leaving civilisation behind, we entered the new unknown world of another undiscovered gorge for us. We were instantly impressed! The beautiful gorge reminded us of the Prasses Gorge near our villa, both equally lovely and with many vivid striations etched into the rock face. Passing by a completely dried up river bed full of varying sizes of boulders and large stones we followed a well-marked red dot wayfarer sign. Many varieties of trees and shrubs thrive here and grow out of the barren rock despite the annual winter floods and torturous summer sun. It was easy walking today with the arid weather conditions but come autumn the heavy and continual rain will come and pour down from the mountains, running in a continuous bubbling torrent and sweeping everything away in its path. Many large branches and even trees and shrubs will be torn out by their roots and carried down into the gorge. Such is the strength and might of the floods, we have seen some battered remains of a car tightly wedged into large boulders from previous years. Today, however; it is peaceful and still and hard to believe such harsh conditions exist, only evident from the flotsam therein.

A few minutes into the walk we began to see the truly magnificent rock-cut caves, with heads tilted back and our eyes screwed up against the glare of the sun we paused to admire their beauty. High above us and framing the blue sky are several birds of prey, be they vultures or buzzards lazily circling and calling out their continuous shrieks; echoing down the otherwise quiet gorge. Further along, we stop to admire a large cluster of wide stripes with different coloured pigmentations in the gorge wall and wonder at such natural beauty. Gnarled and stubby trees stick out at precarious angles growing within the walls, some were being nibbled by a few crazy goats leaning out at a dangerous angle, twenty feet or more above our heads. Although, some don't make it as we have seen evidence of dead goats on other gorge floors which have slipped and fallen to their death!

Stopping now and then to rest we have a drink of water beneath some wild leafy fig trees and remark we hadn't seen another person all day and no one passed us on our return journey, it was as if we were the only ones in the world – so peaceful and quiet. I love the many-coloured stones you see in the gorges and on the beaches, they are quite amazing with such a variety of colours and textures. Towards the end of our outward journey, I saw the loveliest piece of rock which looked a bit like pumice although it was a light creamy colour instead of black. Oval in shape it fitted into the palm of my hand, naturally hollowed out over many years of rainwater pounding its surface, it would have made a lovely finger bowl and I briefly thought about taking it back with us but decided not to.

Having spent our first night in Kato Zakros we decided to drive out of the village and head up onto the top road to find a place to eat because the walk had sharpened our appetite. We intended to drive to the large town of Sitia on the South Coast after our lunch and spend the second night there.

Sitia Town and a Brief History

The town itself is set on a hill tumbling down towards the western end of the picturesque bay of Sitia with its oldest sections hanging steeply above the harbour. The large steps run in a straight line to the very top of the intersections, rewarding us with some beautiful views out towards the sea and the remains of a fortress. The bustling waterfront with many restaurants and tavernas lends a happy atmosphere to locals and visitors alike with a newly constructed promenade leading down to the busy ferry port.

Steeped in history the area was first known as Eteia and may be linked to Minoan times from inscription on some clay tablets with the letters se-to-i-ja written on them. There was a substantial Minoan presence in the area, borne out by the excavations at Petras, the town's southern suburb where a settlement dating to the early second millennium B.C. has been unearthed and where – in later Neo-Palatial period there was an important town with splendid roads and buildings. There is little in way of Roman and Greek influence here although there is an archaeological site of Hellenistic Sitia on the outskirts of the town. The port of Sitia was enlarged and strengthened when the Venetians occupied the area calling it La Sitia.

Reaching the large town of Sitia early evening and parking the car in one of the many terraced streets running parallel to the sea and built into the large hillside. Leaving behind the hustle and bustle from tourists and locals eating and drinking in the busy taverna's we climbed up the steep steps to reach the three different street levels in the quieter part of town. One or two local women passed us as we slowly heaved ourselves up the long steep steps, one old lady dressed head to foot in traditional black and carrying two shopping bags passed us as she steadily climbed up the steps to her home.

"She's fit," I murmured as I watched her pass me by, her little bow legs trotting on at a steady rate. Chris was as breathless as I was and just nodded his agreement.

At the highest point of the town, looking out towards the sea stands a crumbling ruin of what must have once been a beautiful and impressive sandstone fortress. Time ravaged and somewhat neglected, it was purposefully built to protect and shelter the people of Sitia from invaders and pirates of which there had been many down the centuries, leaving their mark to be discovered in later years by teams of enthusiastic archaeologists.

We soon found a delightful Hotel set well back from the promenade in one of the quieter streets. A couple of steps led us into a small shady courtyard with orange trees and sweet-smelling jasmine and underneath, neatly placed, were two or three tables and chairs inviting guests to sit and relax awhile. Knocking on the old wooden door we were greeted by a friendly smiling face who asked us in. The heady scent of jasmine wafted in the warm breeze as we stepped inside the cool tiled hallway. We were shown to the immaculately clean room and facilities and for the price of just 30 euros a night, we were very pleased and comfortable.

Night had fallen by the time we had put our bags in the room and wandered out into the town again to have a relaxing drink and watch the world go by. Always on the lookout for an old traditional taverna, the clues are usually a few elderly Cretan men sitting outside, we found a little bar situated back from the promenade and facing the sea. A small group of local men were sitting talking and having an evening drink as we took our seats at a table in the corner. A few minutes later a young lady brought not only our drinks but three small plates of their home-made mezethes as well. The day had now cooled off and there was a gentle breeze blowing in from the sea. It was very pleasant just sitting and watching people taking their evening stroll, the young men on their scooters or motorbikes with the helmets hanging down the back of their head – speeding along at such a pace and scattering the stray cats scavenging around in the bins.

My attention was drawn to a frail old man sat nursing a small cup of the traditional thick Greek coffee and a tumbler of water, he sat next to us for over an hour just gazing into space, he looked lonely and probably glad of the hustle and bustle of the town. He muttered to himself from time to time, confirming his innermost thoughts. It's Saturday night I thought to myself, the poor man is sitting here on his own, probably no wife and nothing to go back home to, what a shame!

My people-watching was soon broken by Chris asking if I would like another drink. "Why not?" I replied smiling. "It's too early to go back to the room yet, we may as well stay here and enjoy the rest of the evening."

A few minutes later yet another three dishes of assorted meze arrived with our drinks, brought this time by the proprietor himself, a portly guy whose shoulder-length grey curly hair cascaded down the back of his neck. More tasty chunks of freshly cooked chicken and lemon arrived, along with some thick-cut fried potatoes and green beans in tomato sauce and olive oil. This was to be our evening meal, delicious and satisfying.

It was time to wander back to the hotel and take a shower before bed, we were both tired now from walking and sightseeing and it didn't take long before we were both in the land of nod.

It was a lovely Sunday morning and the church bells were ringing out their beautiful melody, calling the local parishioners to come and worship. We wandered along the promenade again looking at all the taverna's facing the sea until we found a suitable place for breakfast. The sun was already hot with a warm gentle breeze blowing in from the sea as we settled down in the comfortable padded wicker chairs and ordered our coffee and pancakes. Once breakfast had settled, we decided to walk up the long steep climb to the ruined Venetian Fortress overlooking the town and take a closer look. It took us just under an hour to walk then stop and catch our breath. Our patience was rewarded with the most wonderful views stretching out before us, the little fishing boats tied up in the harbour in the bay, the colourful tops of restaurant umbrella's, an assorted mix of old and new. We didn't have time to visit the Folklore Museum or the Roman Fish Tanks, but there is always another time, another day.

Picking Arcadi Grapes and Treading Them

3rd Week in September

One morning in September, we went with friends to a large vineyard in the Arcadi Region to pick a field of grapes. Always on the lookout for fun and new adventures we were pleased and excited to help out. We set off at 8:00 am. The early morning sun had begun to warm the air with a promise of another beautiful day. I had made a list the night before what we needed to take with us that morning, sun cream, soap and towel to wash our feet, sunglasses and a broad-brimmed hat for when we were out in the vineyard. We were looking forward to the day ahead because we hadn't done this kind of work before and it would be a unique pleasure. We needed to meet another car en-route so we could travel together in a three-car convoy. Along the dusty narrow lanes, zig-zagging in and out of the tiny villages and hamlets. We eventually turned down a single bumpy track with vineyards on each side of the road and came to a halt outside a gated area to be greeted by a beautiful young Alsatian dog. Wagging her tail and prancing around us, we walked towards a large refrigerated unit with some chairs and a BBQ outside the open door. We were introduced to a charming and friendly couple, Manolis and Litze who owned the two vineyards on each side of the dusty track nearby. We had come well prepared, with some cold bottles of beer for later along with plenty of ice-cold water and soft drinks in our large ice bags. They told us that after the grape picking there would be a big BBQ here with lots of succulent lamb and goat meat, homegrown salad and herbs, home-cooked chips and many other appetisers provided by Manolis and Litze as a thank you.

But first, we needed to collect the juicy bunches of grapes in the two fields, there were ten of us so it shouldn't take too long. The sun was very hot as we plastered ourselves with sun cream, donned our shady hats and gloves to start picking grapes.

"Work along in rows," one Greek guy called out to us, as we collected two large plastic boxes to put the grapes in.

Chris had brought a pair of secateurs with us, but we found we didn't need them because the grapes easily broke away with a gentle tug. It was back-breaking work as these particular vines grow quite low to the ground. Stopping now and then to stretch our back and get a drink of water, we soon finished one field and made a start on the next one by early afternoon.

I think it took us about three hours or so to pick all the grapes and Litze said we had filled 30 large crates and should yield around 400 litres of wine, not bad for a day's work.

We sat in the shade to rest and re-hydrate ourselves underneath a corrugated awning which is attached to the refrigerated unit. Later on, I peeped in to see it was totally stripped out inside. Manolis had made it into a caravan interior with a cloth-covered bench at the far end to either sit or have an afternoon snooze. There were also cupboards, a sink and a preparation area just inside the door, he told us they come to stay overnight in the summer months and watch over their sheep and goats and help with the newborns. He went on to tell us he has a shop in Rethymnon town, making and repairing anything to do with heavy metal, from gates and railing to making BBQ's etc.

Rested and raring to go again, we set off in a convoy of cars and drove into the sleepy hamlet of Agois Antonias stopping outside the little home of Yeorgi, an elderly guy whose twinkling eyes and ready smile made you beam back at him! "It will take place here," he said, pointing down the narrow passageway at the side of his home, "This is where we will be treading the grapes." We carried the overfull crates of large juicy grapes and passed them over the low wall to Yeorgi standing above us inside a deep stone trough. Tipping each one of the 30 crates into the trough, he told us to go and get our feet washed with the hosepipe before climbing inside the trough.

I was buzzing, I couldn't wait – I wanted to be one of the first to begin the steady process of treading grapes as they did in ancient times. I hurriedly pulled my shoes and socks off, standing near the hose to clean my feet and legs with icy cold water before joining two other local guys who had already started pounding the grapes to eventually make the pulp. I was later informed, this slow, ancient process makes for a better wine rather than taking the grapes to a Co-operative to be mechanically pressed.

Chris held my arm as I climbed up on an upturned box, then sitting on the low wall I swivelled myself over and into the trough. It felt strange at first when my feet landed on the stone-cold surface and begin the treading with my feet and toes on the large mountain of juicy pendulous grapes.

Squish, squish, the steady rhythm of three pairs of feet on the soft moist fruit was echoing down the narrow corridor and with it, several faces grinning from ear to ear patiently waiting for their turn to 'have a go'. Some photographs of us were taken inside the trough as I began to do the conga around the stone wall edge, much to the amusement of old Yeorgi who threw his head back and started laughing, showing one or two black stumps inside the open mouth.

Chris eventually took the place of another guy who had decided he had had enough and climbed out. Yeorgi told us when we arrived, "Should you find any snails inside the trough, put them on the wall edge and they will be collected up later." These particular snails have an overall white shell with thin black stripes across them, they are still considered a delicacy to the Cretan people and they cook them in garlic and herbs and toss them in olive oil then eaten straight from the shell using a two-pronged fork. We have tried them in the past when we were both 'spoon fed' by a Cretan Mountain Man on his Naming Day. I managed three before I started heaving but Chris managed a few more out of politeness, it's something we haven't tried eating again! We did hear once that after the German Occupation there wasn't a snail to be had in Crete because the local folk had collected and eaten them regularly as a main source of nourishment. The German soldiers having killed and eaten all their sheep and goats.

More photographs were taken with us holding hands and marching in time to steadily crush the grapes to semi pulp. The liquid was forming now and we were told that the grapes will be left where they were for three days and then crushed again before the liquor was drained off through a hole in the outer wall and into a large container.

I climbed out shortly before the crushing was completed, I had been in there for about half an hour which was long enough. The grapes were very sweet and even though my feet and legs were hosed down again, it didn't clear the sticky residue on them, instead, it attracted wasps and flies. It took several attempts with wet wipes, soap and water from the taverna across the road before the insects would leave me alone. Saying our goodbyes and thank you for letting us come to Yeorgi's home and tread the grapes, we drove back to Manolis and Litze trailer to help at the BBQ.

It was a veritable feast! More meat on the BBQ than any of us could eat. Litze did three lots of chips in virgin olive oil outside on a large wood-burning stove and an equally large metal pan her husband had made. Lots of fresh salads, hot and cold meats, homemade vine leaves and many different appetisers, along with the beer, wine and cordials we all ate together sitting around a huge table Manolis had dragged across for us all to eat in the shade. We laughed and talked about the day's events, cracked jokes, told funny stories, music played and those with still enough energy got up and danced around the table, much to the amusement of the seated audience. We all had lots of fun and laughter, it was such a remarkable and memorable day.

Early evening, very tired and happy, we took our leave with lots of hugs and kisses and the warmest thank you from everyone for such a wonderful experience. We said goodbye to our genial hosts with the promise to see them again soon. Manolis said the wine would be ready at Christmas, taking approximately six weeks from start to finish and they would bring us some to Agia Triada as a thank you for helping them.

Now we were experienced 'hands' we were asked several times to help with picking and weeding grapes by our many friends who have vineyards.

Chapter Seventeen
Kourtaliotiko Gorge

October

When we had done our last walk in The Gorge of the Dead over to the east side of Crete, we longed to do another one almost immediately now the weather had turned cooler and the gorges still quite dry from the long arid summer months – an ideal time for walking in any of Crete's beautiful gorges. We have been told the rains will be coming soon and in October the weather can become unsettled and changeable. In other years we have experienced a lot of heavy rain along with spectacular thunder and lightning during the winter months from October to February, so we knew what to expect.

Chris chose the Kourtaliotiko Gorge due South of the island and one we hadn't walked before, although we had driven along the road which meanders between the solid rock face on each side. Then suddenly the gorge walls rise up so sharply in front of you as you round the bend making it feel you will drive right through and disappear! We see a beautiful shrine cut into the rock face situated high above the narrow road, inviting travellers to stop and climb up the old worn steps to linger a while. Stooping low, we enter into its gloomy interior with just enough room for about three people, the dusty stone altar holds two or three icons and a beautifully framed picture of Christ. A wooden box of tall slender candles and incense are carelessly placed nearby, the rough cave walls are of white emulsion and there is a tiny window ledge with the remains of an old bird's nest. It is eerily quiet and a lot cooler inside, we sit on the only two rush chairs available and enjoy the peace and tranquillity therein.

Soon, we were looking for the path leading down to the bottom of the Kourtaliotiko Gorge to the start of the walk and leave the other tourists behind wearing their flimsy flip-flops and sandals. Sturdy boots with ankle support are a must here if you do not want to damage yourself on loose stones and uneven paths. We always travel in our boots and appropriate clothing when we go walking. Crossing the road again, we slowly descend the steep rough stone pathway until we reached the bottom of the gorge. We could hear fast running water before we could see it and very soon a very lovely waterfall came into view, sparkling and glistening like diamonds in the morning sunlight. There was a complicated, manmade control that held two large metal wheels at the near side of the river. Over on the far bank, we saw a young girl emerging from the river having had her morning bathe in the clear crystalline waters, she reminded me of a beautiful water nymph when she dried her body and her long black hair in the warmth of the day. We turned away and walked left upstream, pausing to admire a natural spring bubbling out of the rocks over on the far side of the bank. Just above was the most beautiful emerald green curtain of lush ferns cascading down in the rock and growing in great profusion from the constant input of clear mountain water which constantly seeped through the porous rock face. We took some lovely photographs of the ferns and the natural mountain springs before moving further down the river bed and onto a border of fine white sand and smooth boulders. A large overhang of mature fig trees gave maximum shade as the warm winds gently rustled through the large leaves casting dappled light and shade across the fast-flowing river. I shuffled forward, stooping low so as not to bang my head on some of the large twisted branches which were dipping low over the river and took a few more photos looking further downstream.

Chris called me over to come and take a look at two tiny crabs hanging onto a green lichen-covered boulder in the middle of the riverbed as the fast-bubbling river water threatened to sweep them away. They appeared to be clinging on with their large crab claws dug deeply into the emerald green moss. "Amazing" moving forward to take a closer look. The crabs were as big as a two-euro piece, their perfectly formed claws were spread out over the moss to stop them from being swept away. I guess they were in the process of catching their lunch. We don't know what their lunch might be. We spent some time communing with nature and with no one else around, no noise, no traffic, only the occasional hum of insects going about their day. I always feel more spiritual on days like this, watching many coloured butterflies and insects, birds and lots of wildflowers – some of which are particular to Crete.

Later, the sun went in, the dark clouds were rapidly descending over the top of the gorge walls and mountains beyond, bringing a sudden chill to the air. The sky changed so quickly from a lovely forget-me-not sky to an ugly grey/white colour, rain was on the way! It was time to walk back down the gorge before the heavy autumn rain came, we had been warned that a bad storm was imminent. The cooler wind blew and the sky grew even darker by the time we reached the car and quickly changed out of our walking boots.

It was only 3:30 pm so after a quick look at the map we decided to follow the Plakias road but instead of dropping down to the coast, we could drive up towards Myrthios via the Kotsifou Gorge. This was new territory for us and we were looking forward to seeing if it was walkable to do another day (not all gorges are suitable or walkable in Crete, sometimes you can only do part of them, sometimes too dangerous to do at all).

The scenic drive through the Kotsifou Gorge was equally beautiful as Kourtaliotiko Gorge. Our attention was caught again to another small shrine cut into the gorge walls so we decided to stop and take a look. We entered through a heavy wooden door; we liked the tiny, narrow wooden windows along with the biggest metal key we have ever seen. The pilgrim is encouraged to lock the shrine doors at all times to give protection from the weather, but also from mountain goats who may decide to wander in and seek shelter for the night.

We drove into the village of Myrthios overlooking the seaside resort of Plakia. By then, the rain was coming down quite heavily and we dashed into the nearest taverna facing the turbulent sea and ordered a drink and something to eat. Chris loves the Greek saganaki and I like kalitsouna, and as they were both on the menu, we ordered them and a cold drink. The rain was thunderous now and we listened to the loud beat pounding on the sunroof above our heads, we were cosy and warm and chatted about our adventures earlier that day.

We were going nowhere; we had brought our books with us in the car and sat reading for a while in the quiet restaurant with only the company of a German couple seated at the far end of the room. As the weather changes here so often in Crete, it brings with it a dramatic change from blue skies and sunshine to an almost negative effect on the hills and mountains when the angry low clouds swirl and mist around the top of the crags, giving an overall surreal effect to the landscape.

We were heading back home and following signs for Rethymnon, passing a lot of major road constructions with part of the new road deviating away from the old one or in part, widening some of the original roads. It will be a lot easier for delivery lorries to bring their goods to the villages as this main road runs from North to South. We are seeing a lot of new infrastructure in Crete with E.U. help, along with household grants to improve living accommodation. Gone are the 'ski jump' toilets (squat and point) and the old lead pipes pouring grimy water into old chipped sinks, modern flush toilets and paper towels instead of shake and drip dry! Although, now and then in mountain tavernas we do still see the odd old-fashioned bathrooms, it all adds to the ambience of Crete.

The Monasteries of Crete
Arcadi Monastery

October

Our pretty little villa nestles in the very toes of the green undulating hills of the Arcadi Prefecture in the North West, with the dramatic Psiloritis Mountains in the distance. With all the neatly kept olive groves and a handful of sleepy old farmhouses and smallholdings, total peace and tranquillity are ever-present; broken occasionally by the piercing cry from a cockerel or barking from a farmyard dog on duty.

To reach the ancient Arcadi Monastery you have a very beautiful car journey through spectacular countryside and only a few kilometres from our home and twenty-three kilometres from the bustling town of Rethymnon. This austere fortress styled Monastery dominates the surrounding cultivated farmland which belongs to and is worked by the few remaining monks, together with some outside help from the local men. Built on a low plateau in the Venetian period it was completed in 1587. It is still totally self-sufficient today as it was on completion centuries ago, with a number of warehouses storing agricultural machinery. The surrounding olive groves and vineyards are also systematically tended by the working monks, producing olive oil and juicy grapes to make the regional Arcadi wine. With sufficient stabling for their horses and donkeys as well as a modern 4 X 4 vehicle to buy provisions in Rethymnon, these dedicated monks go about their daily lives in comparative peace, solitude and prayer.

One early autumn morning in October, we drove from our villa and through the narrow winding roads to visit the monastery. It was a lovely morning with a sharp chill in the air, coupled with the promise of another lovely bright day as the sun climbed high in a forget-me-not blue sky. The hard-working local farmer near our home was already up and about feeding his penned chickens and geese. Slowly passing by his smallholding I wound the window down in the car and listened to the farmer talking to his animals in a deep gruff voice. We stopped the car for a moment to listen to the old man.

"*El-la, el-la, el-la* (come, come here)." This was followed by some indecipherable muttering and then a short pause. A loud cacophony of noise immediately followed with around twenty or more scrawny looking turkeys answering him in their familiar gobble, gobble, gobble sound! The old farmer continued to make a series of affectionate clucking noises to his large flock and they would immediately answer, surrounding him as he threw handfuls of grain in their direction. We decided to get out of the car and take a closer look as the farmer continued the early morning feed to fatten his geese and chickens for Christmas.

"They look in a sorry state, they are so thin and scrawny."

"He must be fattening them up for Christmas, he needs to get as much food down them as possible over the next two months"

Chuckling to ourselves, we returned to the car and continued the journey along the quiet narrow road winding our way up through the olive groves, their ancient branches hanging very low with a bumper crop of olives, ready to harvest later in the year. Vast carpets of vivid yellow flowers from a naturalised wild clover grew in abundance beneath the olive trees, the bright morning sun shone dappled light and shade through the thick twisted branches making a pretty picture. Olive trees can live for hundreds of years and in most regions around Crete they have, what is known as 'monumental olive trees' with the oldest dating between two to three thousand years old!

We were almost at the top of the road and glancing back over my shoulder I looked across to the deep ravine cutting through the middle of our village, dividing the original older property of Agia Triada from the relatively newer homes. Following the line of the ravine it holds large clusters of wild olive trees, oleanders and thick bamboo, eventually meandering out to the vivid blue sea of Rethymnon. Grazing sheep and goats litter the hillside with some perching precariously on smooth jutting rocks high above us to reach the juiciest pieces of herbs, grasses or lichen. Many times, we have seen goats suspended above us whilst out walking in the mountains or gorges, leaning out or edging along a narrow path to nibble at some new growth! As the rocky road levelled out, huge ornate limestone rocks and boulders litter the barren landscape, left behind when the massive shifts from the tectonic plates of the Mediterranean and Atlantic oceans collided to create the beautiful island of Crete and the other smaller island in the Mediterranean and Aegean seas, known as the Hellenic Island Arc.

At last! We catch our first glimpse of the ancient Monastery of Arcadi, the impressive square-shaped buildings are a deep yellow coloured sandstone, vivid in the morning sunlight with high stone walls surrounding them. Local people and travellers were welcomed to shelter here from the various wars and sieges taking place down the centuries. The beautiful entrance was reconstructed and re-built after the explosion of 1866, where to this day you can still see visible evidence of blackened stonework in the southwest corner of the church. The very impressive church stands as a monument to our Lord and the two Saints, Constantine and Helen. The stone covered passageway with row on row of arches is very impressive. One can easily imagine the order of monks being called to prayer, dressed in their familiar brown cassocks and walking slowly in two rows, heads bent in quiet contemplation, their leather sandals shuffling slowly along the shaded cobbled walkways to attend morning prayers and evensong.

The ancient history of Arcadi Monastery goes right back to Byzantine times, approximately 667 B.C. – 1453 B.C. The history book tells us the Monastery was named after the monk Arkadios who originally founded it but we cannot know that for certain. In and around the sixteenth century it was a hive of education with many copyist monks and a rich, well-stocked library and school, as with many other Monasteries on the island. With the advent of the Turkish invasion of 1866, it ceased from being a place of education and turned towards guerrilla warfare against the Turks with the help of three hundred strong and willing men, women and children! Unfortunately, they were greatly outnumbered by the fierce might of the Turkish invaders being 15,000 strong, who stormed the walls of the Monastery and began to systematically slaughter all the men, women and children within. A very brave man who also happened to be the Abbot of Arcadi at that time named 'O. Kostis Giamboudakis' rushed to the gunpowder storage room which is placed at the back of the Monastery setting the wheels in motion which would be forever etched in the history of Crete.

Igniting the large storage of the powder magazine, he produced a massive sky-high explosion, killing himself and all the people who had taken shelter in the Monastery; taking with them a large number of Turkish soldiers as well and reducing large amounts of the Monastery to a pile of rubble. The Monastery now stands as a permanent monument to the Cretan people for liberation and freedom in Crete as well as a solemn reminder of the Ottoman Empire. Large numbers of locals and tourists attend the celebrations which are held in November to remember the courage of the Abbot and all the martyred people who valiantly fought and died there.

A beautiful old tree is situated inside the Monastery's central square, still with a bullet lodged in the bark of the tree, a constant reminder of previous terrorism and siege. Walking further around the immaculate grounds we came upon a well-tended rose garden, each bush held several heady scented blooms ranging from white to pale pink, yellow and deep reds. The various perfumes filled the air and wafted on the warm breeze as we sat down to rest for a while on a wooden bench. Utter peace descended and in quiet contemplation, we listened to many migratory birds chirping and twittering in the branches of the ancient leafy trees surrounding the courtyard.

"I spy a little café over there," I said, grinning at Chris and pointing to an attractive building over at the far end of the grounds, surrounded by wooden decking and holding a few tables and chairs. We wandered over and admired the immaculately farmed land owned and worked by the monks here. We ordered some ice-cold drinks and some delicious Greek yoghurt topped off with home-made Arcadi honey from the local bees here. A small fenced area was partitioned off with a few farmyard animals, ducks, geese, chickens and turkeys. One or two donkeys were together in the next partition and the biggest surprise, further along, were a couple of ostriches, busily fluffing and preening themselves.

"Who would have thought the Monastery would have a couple of ostriches here?"

To our amusement, the ostriches continued to show off and strut their stuff in the clean, well-tended pens as we watched them for a while, fascinated by their antics.

Making our way back over the shady car park, we see an old Greek farmer who has parked his pickup truck under the shade of a large acacia tree and out of the hot sun, he was selling his large juicy oranges which had been freshly picked that morning from his orange groves. We bought a large bagful from him to eat or juice for breakfast the next day.

There is a lot of restoration at the Monastery, encouraging the Greek people and tourists to visit these lovely old buildings and gardens, but also to encourage the Cretan people to make their annual pilgrimage in November. This ongoing and extensive restoration work on such an important and historical building will be preserved for future generations and forever linked to the colourful history of Crete.

Arkadi Monastery to Eleftherna – Six KMS

The Walk

From the route starting point at the Monastery, we followed the tar road signposted Eleftherna-Margarites on the E4 path going the same way. The E4 sign on your right at the beginning of a gravel road going upwards, obstructed by a fence and with a gate, you turn right and then immediately left. Proceed along the rocky sloping path passing by the brushwood, heathers, wild thyme and thorny burnet.

The views on your left side stretch as far as the sea through a typical Cretan landscape with hills and smooth valleys, villages and olive groves, fields and roads. Ascend the gradual slope of the hillside for about fifteen to twenty feet until the path meets an unpaved road. Turn slightly right and down and you will see a small gorge in front of you. Descend into the gully and follow the gravel road, passing by a dilapidated church and an old spring a little way ahead. Cross over the gully and climb to the left onto a goat track, reaching the top (50–60 m ascent) and a gravel road. Pass a fence door and follow the road amongst neatly cultivated fields. A little while later you come to a little church and a much bigger road, turn to the left facing the village's houses and descend to the tar road and the first houses continuing left for nearly 500 m until you come to the centre of the village with a cluster of tavernas and kafenios in the square.

We did this walk in June, it wasn't too hot then and we were very happy to see many wildflowers and herbs along the way. We recommend this walk as it is not too hard and only two hours with lovely views, with the equally beautiful Eleftherna village, gorge and archaeological site as a reward at the end of the walk.

Preveli Monastery

The sharp autumnal morning had a seasonal nip in the air as I tumbled out of bed and flung the shutters back in the kitchen. The bright sunlight flooded into the room and I gazed out at clear blue skies and settled weather, waiting for the kettle to boil for our morning coffee. I heard Chris moving about and called out to him, "What are we doing today? The weather is fine, we should be getting out and about while we can."

Over breakfast, Chris looked through our travel guide book and stopped at the page advertising Preveli Monastery. "We haven't been there before Patti; shall we try this Monastery today?"

On the quiet Armeni road, on our way to Preveli Monastery we saw a 'brown tourist sign' which read 'Late Minoan Cemetery' we parked just outside the double gates leading into the site. We were delighted to see it was still open so late in the year and walked up to the pay booth where a jolly local guy who was sitting behind a desk smiled and waved us into the site without paying.

We learnt that this particular Minoan cemetery had been under excavation since 1969 led by Yiannis Tzedakis who discovered over 200 chamber tombs and one tholos tomb dating from the late Minoan era.

The large impressive chambers are approached by dromoi starting at ground level and descending to the entrance of the tomb by a stone ramp or sometimes stone steps. The original entrances were totally covered by a single large stone, some of which can still be seen just outside the tomb entrance, reminding me of Jesus' tomb in the Garden of Gethsemane. One or two of the larger tombs have a central pillar in the chamber and in at least one tomb there are impressive stone benches carefully cut from solid rock and running along the interior walls.

Many precious items have been recovered including seal stones, jewellery, stone vases and bronze vessels which are now on display in the Rethymnon museum in the town centre.

Over 500 skeletons have also been excavated and with much patient research, a great deal of information has been found on how these people lived, including their diet.

We wandered around for over an hour or so in between the many neat rows of open tombs and noted their approximate length was around ten to sixteen feet long and an average width of five feet at its widest, tapering to three feet nearest to the tomb entrance. The overall site must have been about two acres, with some newly planted trees dotted here and there. Splashes of colour brought some relief to an otherwise austere place as wildflowers and herbs had colonised the rough pasture land.

The largest tomb was placed at the top of the cemetery and heavy metal supports were holding up the roof structure to avoid total collapse. Unfortunately, there wasn't any information as to whose tomb it belonged to but we felt sure it must have been someone important. Nearby, another tomb entrance had a simple line of carving above the entrance and we tried to decipher the inscription as to whose tomb it was. Some other burial tombs had collapsed and the old stone ceiling, grass and earth lay in a large mound in its centre. Several more had two or three inches of stagnant water in the open entrance of the tombs. We were assured this was an important archaeological project and was still an ongoing dig, but it would all amount to time and money at the end of the day to bring the dig to its finality.

Continuing our journey, we followed the signpost pointing towards Plakias as it was heading in the same direction as the Monastery. We drove on some well-surfaced tarmac roads for a while, a unique pleasure over here, and through some sleepy hamlets dotted along the roadside with pretty whitewashed churches, colourful shrines and tiny dolls house dwellings. We were slowly following the road up and leaving behind the last settlement to encounter the next magnificent sight which took our breath away in its natural glory. Ahead of us, we could see that a massive rock face had been blasted away and cut through its belly to make the road we see today. As the road wound its way on a sharp right-hand bend, suddenly! The high and mountainous rock face rose up to meet us, threatening to swallow us whole.

An involuntary 'Ohhh!' emitted from me as Chris lightly pressed the brakes – "I thought the road was going to disappear into the gorge." We pulled into a layby further along the road to stop and admire the fantastic views. The cold icy air hit us as we got out and walked over to the edge of the fenced-off layby and looked down into the river bed, bubbling and breaking over massive boulder stones. We were totally surrounded on each side of a high sided rock face, deeply etched with various beautiful hues of blue, green, grey and brown. Straining our necks to look up to the highest peaks we watched several buzzards lazily circling on the autumn thermals and making their familiar mewling noises. The strong winds were being channelled through the natural wind tunnel and we held onto each other for support to stop us from being blown off our feet. We had to shout above the strong gusting winds which threatened to take our breath away. The gorge sides were so high it made us feel dizzy when our eyes searched every bit of this impressively natural phenomenon, giving us the strangest feeling of being so small compared to the huge and powerful might of such fantastic beauty. I think we uttered more 'wows' and "Oh, look at that" in the space of twenty minutes than we did for the rest of the day! It was awesome and mind-blowing.

Pressing on, we left the impressive canyon behind on our journey towards Plakias, a popular seaside resort in the summertime, but now it was a quiet sleepy place with just the local people and one or two 'late comers' like ourselves. From the summit, we paused to look down on the pretty little bay with its shuttered gift shops, tavernas and restaurants neatly dotted around the sparkling blue Libyan Sea. On a motorised helter-skelter, we coasted down the tarmac road and parked on a wide expanse of stone gravel near the beach to walk along the seashore. One or two local fishermen were doing some remedial repairs on their fishing boats or mending the nets. One or two beach bars were still open trying to tempt the passer-by to come and sit inside their gazebo facing out to sea and relax with a drink. Instead, we decided to stretch our legs and stroll along in the afternoon sunshine, relaxed and happy to enjoy a spot of beachcombing along the fine, pale golden sand and listen to the sparkling blue sea gently lap along the edge of the shoreline. A light wind blew in from the sea with many white scudding clouds racing along the pale blue skies. This is heaven I murmured, as I collected some tiny coloured stones which were washed up onto the beach, to make another beautiful mosaic picture on canvas.

Over at the far end of the beach and well away from the shops and tavernas we watched two young rock climbers slowly scaling the rock face, high above the road leading out of Plakias. One climber was safely roped and hooked into his belt as he encourages his pal to follow him. Whether the second climber was relatively new to the art of rock climbing we didn't know but he appeared to be stuck and couldn't move one way or another up the craggy rock face. Swinging this way and that like a pendulum, he tried to secure a firm foothold but to no avail and eventually, he shouted up to his pal he was going to climb back down again – which they both did!

"Phew! That was a trial," I said to Chris as the boys abseiled down and got their feet on terra firma again. Turning back again and walked towards the marina, wondering why some people take the risk of the mountain or rock climbing as a hobby.

We followed the coast road indicating the way to Preveli Monastery, just five kilometres now, we drove past many olive groves where sheep and goats grazed under the leafy shade of the gnarled branches. One or two goats had strayed onto the highway totally oblivious to passing traffic as they cropped the juicy grasses at the side of the road and following close behind were their cute kids. The road began to slowly wind up through the groves and away from the sea for a while, it was then we saw the old abandoned Monastery with its crumbling walls now partially covered in wild re-growth as nature had reclaimed the land. Sadly, neglected and unloved, it was too dangerous to view the ruins at close quarters, we could only look through the padlocked iron gates at the crumbling remains of what once would have been a large productive Monastery. This was the first Preveli Monastery of St John the Theologian comprising of two main building complexes, the ruined lower Monastery of St John the Baptist which was eventually abandoned from continual raids from pirates coming in from the Libyan Sea, stealing the Monastery's gold, jewels and religious artefacts. Later a new Monastery of the same name was securely constructed on higher ground, this was the one we were about to visit.

The Monastery was founded around the Middle Ages during the occupation of Crete by the Republic of Venice. It slowly developed over several centuries as a religious and cultural centre, absorbing amongst many others – the Ottoman invasion. In 1821, the Abbot led a group of rebels in the Greek War of Independence where extensive damage occurred to the Monastery to be later rebuilt and restored. The Monastery was once again instrumental in organising rebellions against the Turks which led to Crete's independence and the ultimate union with Greece.

In the Battle of Crete 1941, the Monastery offered unconditional help to the British and ANZAC soldiers providing food and shelter to the men. As a consequence of this, a group of Australian soldiers managed to secure their escape from the island at nearby Previli beach. The German forces were outraged and as a reprisal they purposefully destroyed the Lower Monastery. The new Monastery holds many precious religious relics and icons and many of its buildings have now been fully restored.

We continued following the road leading up to the new Monastery until we actually 'ran out of road'. The beautiful Monastery buildings are perched at the very top of the hillside with magnificent views all around us. It felt like we were on top of the world as we gazed out over the steep undulating pastures where the Monastery's sheep and goats grazed far below us. We entered the pretty cobbled courtyard surrounded by the well-maintained Monastery buildings, a few well-fed lazy cats dozed in the afternoon sunshine, some stretched out on benches and others were sleeping in the cool shade of the sandstone walls.

A lovely memorial stone dominated the central square, elevated by six stone steps with a large brass plaque praising the courageous Abbott who helped the English, Australian and New Zealand soldiers to leave Crete safely by boat during the German occupation.

The afternoon was fast drawing to a close and it was too late for us to 'knock on the wooden door' to see inside the church and museum. We had lingered too long at the other places along the way, so we had run out of time to look around the Monastery but there would be others days when we could come and do it justice.

Something else we missed too as we were walking back to the car, we heard some animal noises coming from behind a high stone wall. Standing on tiptoe we could just about see a few animals in the yard below us. There were peacocks, geese and a beautiful young deer with magnificent antlers, a smart aviary with colourful parakeets screeching and chattering. We left as quietly as we came and turning back to look over my shoulder, I see the neat rows of monks' cells situated in an area where colourful shrubs and flowers were happily growing and well-tended by the Monks of the Holy Order.

It was a slow and careful drive back down the steep winding helter-skelter road, enjoying the stunning views again and returning home again through the immaculately kept agricultural land of Preveli Monastery.

Chapter Eighteen
Prassanos Gorge

Thumbing through one of our walks books one evening, we found another walk which hadn't been done before, through the Prassanos Gorge.

The Prassanos Gorge is Located ten kilometres South-East of Rethymnon; an awe-inspiring and inviting sight as it carves a swathe through the countryside to the coast by Rethymnon. It has been created by some great force as you will see from the massive boulders en route. The landscape around is very open and pleasing to look at, making a good accessible walk. A walk between April and October through gigantic rocks situated next to the barren hills of Gargana and populated with buzzards and a few Bonelli's eagles, you may be lucky enough to observe the last four remaining couples of Griffon Vultures that nest in this area. Its cliffs are huge and imposing with its inaccessible caves high above, it is an ideal nesting place for vultures. I retrieved the walks book later and found further interesting information which told me that botanists consider this particular area just as important as the famous Samaria Gorge. The Cretan gorges were first formed in the late Miocene period around five to ten million years ago, the intense uplift of the whole Cretan area was due to plate tectonics rising to form many interesting gorges, caves and plateaus. The gorges are formed mainly in carbonate rocks i.e., limestone and marble as a result of land uplift and erosion by water from the rivers. The land uplift is usually caused by 'faults' or cracks in the earth. Very informative and interesting.

We packed the rucksack and prepared refreshments before we went to bed that evening so we could be up and out early to begin our walk. There were so many things we needed to pack for every eventuality, jumpers, thin waterproofs, boots, map and compass, first aid kit, mosquito repellent, sun cream and sunglasses, mobile phone, picnic and plenty of iced water. I started putting a 'post-it' reminder on the fridge/freezer to tick-off everything we needed.

Parking the car by the side of the quiet road we pulled on our walking boots, grabbed our sun hats and rucksack then advanced down a rough dirt path towards the yawning giant's mouth of the Prassanos Gorge. The book had warned us that there were lots of massive river bed stones and the terrain will be very uneven underfoot with the risk of twisting or even breaking your ankle if you do not remain vigilant (a good start!). As any serious walker knows, a pair of good walking boots which cover the top of your ankles are a must and help enormously.

Leaving the sloping dirt road and onto the uneven concrete track, we paused for a moment to admire the large mouth of the Prassanos Gorge. Walking at a steady pace and passing through an old wire goat fence, we followed another rough track which led us out onto an elevated ridge surrounded by a sea of tall green ferns growing on each side of the narrow goat track. We were now descending at a moderate pace, enjoying the wonderful views as the book had promised – 'the landscape is very open and pleasing to look at'. A familiar mewling sound of six or seven buzzards was circling high above our heads like tiny dots set against a beautiful blue sky. The warmth of the sun shone through the huge old plane trees, lining our route along the little path, throwing spears of dappled light onto the massive rocks and smooth boulders where they had laid for millions of years in the dry riverbed. No rain had fallen for eight months now, coupled with continuous hot sunshine since February the sunken riverbed was totally devoid of any moisture whatsoever.

At last, we were walking into the giant's mouth at the very entrance of the gorge, pausing now and then to gaze at the impressive rock formations. Eventually, the beautiful gorge opened out before us, we looked up at the massive towering sides and the multi-coloured striations of blue, red, brown and greens merging into each other to form an exquisite abstract picture.

The quiet hush was interrupted by a constant tinkling of bells coming from further down the gorge, it was the familiar sound of bells strung around the goats' necks, and herding the goats towards us at a fast pace were two large dogs. My stomach turned over and I hid behind Chris until he had accessed the situation. Meanwhile, the dogs did not alter their pace but continued to leap over large rocks as they quickly advanced towards us. We have had some prior experiences with farm dogs in England and Crete when we have been out walking, some can be nasty and will bite you if they think you are trespassing on their master's property.

As the two dogs got nearer to us, they stopped suddenly and watched us watching them – stalemate!

"Now, what do we do?" I whispered in Chris' ear, still standing behind him. "Nothing, just wait," came the whispered reply as we both stared back at the puzzled dogs.

A minute or two went by then one dog started slowly moving forward, climbing up the rocks and well away from the path we were on. The other dog followed behind and carefully picked their way over the stones while they continued watching us. As they drew level, they gave us one last look and surged forward to catch up with the herd of goats. We thought the goats were probably being taken for milking, and with the dogs being so well trained they could be sent out at the same time every day without the farmer.

Peace and quiet reigned once more with the exception of the rustling leaves, stirred gently by a warm breeze blowing down the gorge. It felt like we were the only two people left on earth, the gorge gave the strange impression we had zoomed back to a time when dinosaurs roamed the earth. It felt as if we would see a tyrannosaurus around the next curve in the gorge, stretching its long neck up to eat the juicy leaves in the canopy of trees. Over many years of walking Crete's fantastic gorges, we have never had this strange sensation before or since.

Laughing and talking about feeling this strange phenomenon we began to notice our voices bouncing and echoing off the massive gorge walls.

"Hello!" I called out to no one… Hello… Hello… Hello… hhh. The facsimile of my voice replied. "I do like this," I said and started laughing, then my laughter echoed around the gorge.

As we proceeded down the path and along the riverbed, it became difficult when the smaller stones and pebbles gave way to a series of much larger rocks and boulders. Still passable, we paused now and then to admire many beautiful multi-coloured rocks and on a closer look, we could see many natural mineral deposits deeply melded into them. Many strange colours and unusual shapes had been formed by the passage of time, beaten by the hot sun and annual rainfalls, the torrential winter rain and snow pouring down from the mountainside and pummelling the limestone rocks to form many magnificent abstract shapes, some like animals and birds.

The faint tinkling of goat bells became louder and louder as we picked our way over the flotsam and jetsam along the narrow pathway. We could smell them long before we could see them, around thirty or more large mountains goats;

their long shaggy coats in various hues from shades of cream to brown and black, grazing on anything they could find in the cool shadows of the gorge walls. Many nannies had their kids with them and stopped eating, curiously watching us as we slowly walk by so as not to frighten them. A few large, impressive Billy goats, taller than the rest, staring unblinkingly at us with their strange eyes. Some Billy goats had very ornate curly horns which corkscrewed around their heads and over their face, giving them an almost comical appearance. These were Cretan mountain goats.

Even further down the gorge, we began to notice how much cooler it had become as the gorge walls were still higher than before, engulfing us from the heat of the day. Swinging ninety degrees along the stony path we came across the biggest pure white boulders we have ever seen, blocking our way, it looked like a giant had heaved them over in a fit of rage – they were so high, pile upon the pile. It appeared to be the end of our walk unless we had the added energy and strength to rock climb over them. Apart from that, it wasn't safe to try climbing over them with being so far away from civilisation. However, it was a good time to rest and eat our picnic, we found a suitable place in the shade and perched on one of the smooth boulders. Busily munching our delicious sandwiches, we searched the spaces in between the rocks to look at various bits and pieces of debris that were tightly wedged in from previous high floods. Lots of tiny bugs and pretty emerald green mosses and tiny flowers had made their home here over the dry summer months and held our attention as we finished the picnic.

It was mid-afternoon when we started back up the gorge, the nights were drawing in as it was almost the end of October. They do not have twilight in Crete so it was prudent to begin our return journey in daylight hours. On our return journey, we enjoyed the beautiful gorge just as much as when we had walked it earlier, stopping now and then to run our hands over the ultra-smooth and intricately patterned rocks and boulders.

"This Prassanos Gorge – This beautiful island of Crete – is a geologist and botanist's delight, a dream come true," I tried to freeze-frame all the wonderful colours in the rocks and boulders and gorge walls. Sometimes, I have difficulty in finding the right words to describe the many beautiful and awe-inspiring places we have seen in Crete, but I sincerely hope that my humble efforts will help the reader imagine how delightful all these places are.

Gradually ascending out of the cool interior of the gorge, the late afternoon sunshine warmed our bodies as we headed back through open pastures and towards the narrow ridge. A small herd of goats were grazing, scattered around the rough scrubland as we approached them on the narrow track. Ahead of us was a jet-black nanny goat about to give birth to her young, we came to an abrupt halt so we didn't frighten or disturb her. She was standing on the path we would take to return home, with a sheer drop into the lower field to our left and a very steep rock face to our right side, we couldn't do anything else but wait and watch her.

Walking back a few metres, we found a place to rest and wait until she gave birth to her firstborn right there in front of us! Immediately, she busied herself fussing, licking and nudging the tiny kid to get up and start suckling her. With wobbly legs and a few flops down on the path the little goat eventually managed to suckle its mother. We were stunned and delighted with such an unexpected experience and felt privileged to have witnessed this miracle. It brought tears to my eyes when the frail kid made little mewling noises to its mother as she carefully licked its face clean of the membrane. It left us almost speechless when another kid was born a few minutes later and with a resounding plop, it landed on the dusty track next to its sibling who was becoming stronger now. We could see that the second kid wasn't strong, it wasn't making any survival attempts to either get up or make the same mewling noise to attract the mother, so the nanny goat gave her full attention to the firstborn and totally ignored the weaker one.

We continued watching, then a further ten minutes or so had lapsed and her 'after birth' came away in a neat 'whoosh'. She attended to herself then, eating the afterbirth and licking herself clean whilst keeping a watchful eye on us and her kids. Then from nowhere, a dozen or more nanny goats took the opportunity to walk past us in single file and went towards the new mother and her kids. They then slowed down to inspect and say hello to the two newborns before continuing along the path and down into the field to resume their grazing.

"Well, I've never seen anything like that before, have you, Chris?"

Chris looked at me and in a serious tone of voice replied "The second kid is very weak; it will probably be dead by morning."

We looked across at the poor frail creature whose head had now lolled on one side, the mother had moved away to let her strong firstborn suckle her again. With the absence of shade and purposeful neglect from the mother I knew Chris was right but it still made me feel sad to see nature in the raw.

Time was marching on and the sun was beginning to set, sinking low behind the trees. There was a quiet stillness within the remaining warmth of the day and we knew we would have to try and edge past the new mother very carefully so as not to frighten her and abandon her young.

I edged my way along with my back to her so she won't feel threatened. Each measured sideways step, inch upon inch until we reached over to the other side of them. We must have scared her a little bit when she moved onto some loose shale rock just above the path and away from her family. Now and then we turned to look over our shoulder to check she was alright, each time we did we saw her watching us from a distance.

Talking about it over dinner later that evening, we felt it had been a very special day, not only a good day's walking but a privilege to have witnessed the birth of new life.

Petras Bridge

It was now November and the weather had changed considerably, so when we saw the sun peep through the heavy storm clouds with a break in the rain, we decided to wrap up well in thick coats, hats and wellingtons and drive to one of our favourite beaches, situated just the other side of Rethymnon, the pretty Petras Bridge. A particularly fierce storm had recently thrown up lots of flotsam and jetsam onto the beach along with some handy-sized pieces of driftwood for our fire. We stood watching the large crashing waves throwing tremendous amounts of black seaweed onto the pebbled shoreline, making the turbulent sea almost black as it bubbled and boiled with its enormous power.

"The holidaymakers don't see it like this," I shouted above the roaring sea and strong powerful winds. We spent a happy hour or so collecting wood and doing a bit of beachcombing, it's surprising what you find on the beach during a heavy storm. We have found some thick coiled rope and orange floats which must have been washed over from a fishing boat, flip flops, bucket and spade, a few sea birds, a sheep! Many pieces of ornate olive and acacia wood, ornately curled in a pleasing fashion. Some of my finds have been put in our garden as ornaments, alongside the magnificent goat's head Chris found when we were walking in the Psiloritis Mountains.

I do love this pretty little beach with its cluster of black jagged rocks and tiny inlets rising up from the sea, occasionally we see black cormorants spreading their wings in a curved manner to seek shade from the sun and watch below for fish. Our attention was drawn away from the beach combing to watch an enthusiastic fisherman who had climbed over a few sharp rocks jutting out of the turbulent sea with his fishing tackle, he was precariously balanced on the very edge of the angry sea as it swirled and crashed around him. He cast his line into the sea and waited patiently for a catch, sometimes the strong winds caught his body making him sway about.

"Have you seen the cloud formations on the mountains, Patti?" I turned my head away, initial concern for the fisherman forgotten as my eyes fell on the strikingly beautiful views of the Lefka Ori mountain range. A light dusting of snow had fallen overnight onto the high peaks, and as the morning sun shone down it gave the appearance of icing sugar, sparkling and shimmering in the morning sunlight. Just below the peaks, a dense blue-grey cloud mass hung low, suspended around the lower parts of the mountains. A little while later, the moody clouds began to lift and part, it looked for all the world like theatre curtains. The sun shone even brighter in a light blue sky, then the magnificent White Mountains took centre stage!

Monumental Olive Tree at Ano Vouves

As I mentioned earlier in the book regarding the Monumental Olive Trees on the island, there is none as old and stately as the beautiful olive tree in the sleepy village of Ano Vouves, and one fine day early in November we decided to drive out and take a look for ourselves. Our walks book tells us the tree is famous throughout Greece, a piece of living history and it has seen the zenith of Minoan Crete. The gnarled and contorted tree looks every one of the 4,000 plus years attributed to it by experts from the University of Crete. Having suffered in recent years as a dog kennel, it is still producing a mass of leafy foliage and an extensive amount of olives, it was rightly rescued and is now a source of pride in the village of Ano Vouves. In 2004, a branch was carried to Athens by a reconstructed Minoan boat, and two victory wreathes were fashioned from its leaves to honour the first and last winners in the events of the Olympic Games in Athens.

Turning off the National Road we were driving through many olive groves where men, women and children were busily working together spreading large black nets under the base of each tree. The olive harvest would be in a few weeks, the women and children will gather the fallen olives from the nets. The men will use either a stout bamboo cane as they have always done from time immemorial or a modern battery-powered thresher to beat and shake the olive branches. The workers stopped for a moment to watch us go by, calling out and waving. The constant thwacking noise of the vibrating beaters began again, dislodging the olives to fall down onto the nets where they would be loaded into the back of their pickup trucks. They will then take them to 'a co-operative' building, where they would be weighed before being processed into their finest virgin olive oil, some days later the farmer would return to the building to collect his share. The large 'queen' olives are for eating and the smaller ones are used for oil. All olives taste very bitter and inedible when they are collected, so the farmer crushes them first and then steeps the olives for three days in fresh water, changing the water each day. Our friend Savvas showed Chris how to do the process with the green olives growing by the side of our villa, they used a large stone to crush them and when they had finished, they had large splatters of olive oil down the front of their shirts. We took the processed olives back with us that year for Christmas, needless to say, they were delicious!

Further down the narrow lanes and just outside the village of Rodopos we got out of the car and watched two guys busily hauling their nets out of a pickup and into the olive grove, I asked them if I could take a photograph for my book and they agreed, posing and smiling still holding the heavy nets in their hands. They seemed flattered to be asked and said 'maybe we will see our picture in your book one day.

Entering the quiet sleepy village of Ano Vouves, now famous and visited regularly by tourists from all over the world to come and marvel at the ancient olive tree, and visit the newly built museum nearby. The beautiful olive tree dominates the very centre of the village and drew us to its presence. Slowly and reverently we walked up to the massive monument, some of the large branches were being held up with steel poles. We thought it would take three adults – holding hands, to entirely circle its massive trunk. I ventured closer and looked up at the leafy canopy above my head, slowly stretching my arms around the massive girth. I pressed my cheek against the rough bark of the tree, closing my eyes I whispered my thoughts to this fine old gentleman. If you can feel pity for a tree, I did that day when we walked around its four and a half metre base. This beautiful old tree was completely hollow inside, a few years ago a local family in the village dug the middle out to make a dog kennel! As Chris took some photographs, I stroked and patted the most remarkable tree I have ever seen. I am not ashamed to say I am a 'tree hugger'.

Returning to the main road and out of the village, we decided to see how far we could drive up 'one of the fingers' of Crete named the Rodopos Peninsular. We were soon in a bleak wilderness with only a few sheep and goats for company. The steep rocky hillsides were unsuitable for the olive farmers, being haphazardly covered with a large amount of limestone rocks, wild gorse, sage and sparse vegetation along with the familiar sharp prickly shrubs. Totally unsuitable for walking, the sheep and goats seemed quite happy to pick around the sparse, rocky landscape and graze along the extensive bleak, barren wasteland.

Passing through the picturesque hamlet of Afrata and along a very narrow road, curving around the walls of some pretty whitewashed houses – jutting out at peculiar angles along its length. We slowed right down and almost stopped completely as the narrow road disappeared, to be replaced with a small path leading up to someone's front door. Of course, we should remember that when the villages were originally built many years ago, no motor cars existed, the only form of transport was a donkey and cart or pedestrians. The tight huddle of buildings would protect the village from the extreme weather conditions. There are also old villages built this way in some parts of England in many coastal towns and fishing villages.

Leaving the protected hamlet behind, we drove slowly along the bumpy track with loose stone and potholes. The temperature was quickly dropping with a cold wind blowing inside the car as we ventured even higher. When the cold winter weather comes it will become uncomfortable and isolated here, and we wondered how the local people made a living in some of the remote villages because it didn't seem fit for habitation.

I looked over at the tiniest whitewashed church set into the mountainside above us, built on a large jutting rock overhanging a deep gorge and wondered how you could get there. Turning onto another rough uneven road we drove as far as we could go, with no civilisation whatsoever, not even a stray sheep or goat, no trees or anything growing there. We got out of the car and were met by a cold howling wind whipping around us. No birdsong, no bleating of sheep and goats, nothing – just the constant eerie sound of the low moaning wind.

"It's incredible," I shouted to make myself heard above the howling wind. "It makes you feel like we are the only people here on earth – it's so bleak and isolated."

We were hoping to be able to follow the road right up to the very top of the peninsular and continue along a further 15 kilometres on the bumpy uneven track, unfortunately, the track deteriorated further and became only fit for walking or driving slowly in an 'off the road' vehicle.

On the return journey home the evening sun was magnificent as it began to set over the mountains casting a lovely peachy pink glow onto the recently fallen snow covering the mountain peaks. Then the darkening sky became streaked with varying hues of purple, reds and scarlets. Reminding me of a beautiful poem I would like to share with you.

Red and smouldering evening sky,
Two alters now before you lie.
One of earth, its loves and sins,
And one of greater whole.
Heaven in our hearts and souls.

Your colours fail to fade away,
As sunset falters on the day.
But rest beyond our conscious view,
To come to us as Godhead rules.
Our hearts and souls again to bless.

And they pass to inner slopes,
And mountain vales of every kind.
To hills and cliff sides of our minds,
Where we can pause for sunset rest.
When sated by our daily haste.

BY; E. ZIMMERLI.

Chapter Nineteen
Our Friends and Neighbours

November

We were fast approaching the end of this year's holiday and very soon we would be packing everything away and covering the furniture with dust sheets until next April. We usually catch the very last flight out of Heraklion to Manchester when everything closes down and Crete belongs to the Cretan people once more.

We woke to bright sunshine and an almost cloudless sky and I walked out onto the patio by the pool with a large mug of coffee in my hand, breathing in the fresh morning air. I listened to the birds singing in the olive grove behind our villa along with the occasional cockerel crowing from a local farm until it was time for breakfast.

Later that morning we decided to take a little walk from our home, packing the rucksack we set off down the dirt track road to begin the walk. Passing by our friends, George and Maria's house, their little dogs yapped and wagged their tails to greet us, the smallest one of the three tethered to a dog kennel that had started life as an oil drum. One of the beautifully plumed cockerels strutted past us, on his way to keep the smallest dog company. When darkness falls and the temperature drops, we see one of the cockerels cuddling up to the little dog inside his kennel!

"Do you think smallest dog minds sharing his kennel with Mr Cockerel?" I said one evening on our way back from a day's walking.

"I don't think the dog has many choices, Chris replied, the cockerel probably bullies him, you can see how he pushes the dog to the front of the kennel whilst he snuggles down behind him."

Pausing for a moment we stood looking across to the olive groves which had been planted a few years ago in neat rows, sloping away to the bottom of the gorge. We have made some good friends with our neighbours who live a short distance away in the older part of the village, there is an ancient lady called Katarina of indeterminate age, very thin and frail and permanently bent over from many years of constant hard work on the land and poor living conditions. When she smiles her little face lights up with such a warm and welcoming greeting, revealing her last remaining tooth at the front of her mouth. Her daughter-in-law lives a short distance away from her and we often see them taking an evening stroll down the quiet lane before sunset, sometimes with a thick blanket or duvet wrapped around their shoulders. Living in the same large house as the daughter-in-law is her sister Maria, we call her 'Mrs Smiley' for obvious reasons. Whenever she sees us her lovely face lights up into a wide happy smile and she often waves to us to stop and come up to the house where we are greeted in a typical friendly Cretan tradition. Hugging and kissing us both, she chatters away in her native language, it always takes a lot of concentration to understand her but with a lot of gesticulating, nodding heads and laughing we can usually get through. The Cretan people are very warm-hearted and generous and we sometimes have little gifts pressed into our hands when we say our goodbyes, it could be a dozen fresh eggs from their hens or a big bag of juice oranges from their orchard, or delicious first press olive oil from their groves, we try to reciprocate by giving gifts too.

One morning when we were returning from a walk we passed by George and Maria's farmhouse, they were sitting on their terrace in the shade of the pergola, they waved for us to come and join them. Hugs and kisses were exchanged and we sat down with them to catch up on the news. Maria went into the house and came out a few minutes later with a large tray of fresh coffee and some tasty homemade biscuits. We spent a happy hour or so chatting and enjoying each other's company and as we were leaving, Maria beckoned Chris to follow her to a holding pen with several large rabbits they had bred for the table. Maria picked out a large healthy rabbit and gave it to Chris to kill, skin and joint and have later for our dinner. She knows Chris was a butcher and has his slaughtering knives back at the villa, so it wouldn't be much trouble to prepare the rabbit. I made a rabbit stew with fresh vegetables from the market in Rethymnon that evening and invited friends around to share it with us. It was the first time they had ever eaten rabbit and enjoyed it as much as we did.

Another day, another year, George asked Chris if he would help him kill an old nanny goat for him, he said she could no longer have kids and couldn't produce milk. He added that as her 'paps' was dragging on the ground, he was afraid she could get an infection in them and he didn't want that. Chris went around at an appointed time with his knives and met up with George and Costa, Maria's cousin to help him. The job was done quickly and cleanly without any stress to the goat, and the three of them hoisted the goat upside down so Chris could skin it. They watched Chris for a while, George said they skin animals a different way in Crete than how he was doing it. Chris cut the goat down the middle and peeled it back over the legs, whereas the Cretan men would cut it around the feet and actually pump air between the inner skins to loosen the pelt. This is an ancient tradition applied in Crete and probably other countries, then they tie the pelt legs together and use the skin to carry water or maybe oil. This was useful in the mountains for the goat or sheep farmers to be able to carry their fresh water on their shoulders while tending to their herd.

Walking at a leisurely pace in the warm morning sunshine along the quiet roads leading towards the tiny hamlet of Agias Dimitrios, we pass by some farm machinery and concrete storage shelters for the pigs. There are always one or two farm dogs chained up and bark constantly to let you know they are doing their job. Today was no exception, the only difference was that the smaller of the two dogs appeared to have lost its voice with too much barking, because when it opened its mouth to bark at us walking by only a loud croak came back for its trouble and sometimes nothing at all! I think the dog must have felt it was a waste of time, he eventually gave up croaking at us and started walking towards us wagging its tail.

The little narrow road continued winding its way down to the bottom of the gorge valley, passing through neat plantations of olive, lemon and orange groves, the beautiful smell of orange blossom in springtime is quite heady; filling the air with a strong sweet smell. We paused to admire the spectacular views of the verdant gorge which runs just below our villa and out to sea. Passing by the elevated pig farm on our right we could hear the sound of pigs grunting and squealing from inside the large concrete piggery, they will be enjoying their pig swill breakfast. Soon, we were coming into the village of Agias Dimitrios with a few old traditional villas lining the route along the outskirts of the village. A few homes were fenced off with sizeable plots of land, growing a vast amount of vegetables and fruit for their own culinary use. One or two dwellings had well-established grape vines trailing over wooden pergolas by the front door, some with shrivelled remains of black grapes still attached to the vines. Unusual Mediterranean shrubs and flowers framed the stone paths leading to their front door, others had several terracotta pots which held brightly coloured geraniums of deep red, pink and white, growing in a colourful tangle and tumbling over the sides.

Following the old wooden signpost to the village centre, we heard some tinny Greek music and a man wailing at the top of his voice which was coming from a loudspeaker attached to a battered pickup truck parked further down the lane. Now and then the deep voice of the farmer would shout out to advertise his fruit and vegetables a few local women waited to be served. We decided not to walk through the village after all with so much noise going on, as by then, a few tethered dogs had joined in the fun as we escaped through the narrow streets where the high walls around the villas echoed with a dreadful cacophony of human and dogs.

Following the signpost on the main road towards Loutra village and nearby Pigi (pronounced Peeyee) village, there are some old traditional villas around the main square with the newer homes being summer apartments and villas named Pigi Paradise. Turning towards the homeward stretch, we had been walking for about two hours now. Passing by a popular local taverna, now closed for winter and situated in the outskirts of the village, several pickup trucks passed us by loaded down with large cut branches from their olive groves, with one or two trucks carrying the cuttings of thick bamboo and leafy foliage for animal feed or fencing.

Fires can be lit on farm land from September right through until April to burn unwanted rubbish from their olive groves and fields. We have helped clear land in fields and underneath the olive trees a few times for our friends over the years to end the working day with a lovely outdoor BBQ and cold beers. One day when we were helping our friend Savvas, we saw one of his men pile one of several bonfires branches up so high it instantly caught fire to another large olive tree. The smoke and flames were shooting high in the air in a matter of seconds, and Chris shouted over to him to do something quickly; with a stupid grin on his face, he picked up the large chain saw and chopped the burning branch off the tree, then he picked up a fallen palm branch and began to beat the remaining flames out until it lay smouldering on the ground.

"No problem here," he shouted over to us grinning, and then he resumed cutting and dragging more branches over to another bonfire further down the field.

"Blimey, he's a pyromaniac," I muttered to Chris as we carried on helping Savvas with the work.

Fires that get out of control are a regular problem in Crete; we have seen the destruction from many large fires over the years here, with some threatening life and limb. Two years ago, there was a really bad fire on each side of the busy National Road heading towards Chania; it took them a long time to put the fire out using sea water bombs dropped by helicopter. Amazingly, it missed a large petrol station at the side of the road, the strong winds had fanned the fire around the back of the petrol station and narrowly missing what would have been a massive explosion. The enquiry said the fire was from a carelessly discarded cigarette. A few properties were damaged, along with a small pine forest and several mature eucalyptus and palm trees.

Following the main road back to our villa, the last leg of our walk is a gradual climb up the lanes, which lasted for another hour or so, hard going now as the midday sun beat down on us and once we arrived back at the villa, we were quite happy to sit in the shade and relax until it was time for dinner.

The Tomb of the Five Virgins

Early morning brought with it another cloudless blue sky, I leapt out of bed full of anticipation and flung the shutters back in the bathroom, revealing one of the best views you could wish for. An old but well-tended olive grove is situated just over a low stone wall in our garden and often filled with a few sheep or goats grazing on the lush clover grass and herbs beneath the trees. An ancient carob tree is at the far end of the field with its massive branches extending out and hung with black pods of carob nuts; these are fed to the animals as a good source of nourishment. Framed in the distance against an azure blue sky are the foothills of the Psiloritis Mountains, always changing colour and textures along with interesting and varied cloud formations.

We thought we would do another walk because we were nearing the end of our holidays. The weather was settled for now, but it could change again and get a cold wind and heavy rain.

Boots, map and compass – we were off! Heading towards the Atsipopouli Interchange on the National Road which runs along the top of the island. As it was early November, most of the crowded beaches were deserted, along with cafes, tavernas and restaurants closing up for the winter on a daily basis. Soon we were leaving the fast road behind and following the winding roads through a series of villages and hamlets to see some of the local families coming out of church having attended a Sunday service. A small group of smartly dressed ladies wearing black jackets and skirts with matching shoes and bags were stood in a group talking by the doorway of the church, exchanging pleasantries before going home to make Sunday lunch for their family. It is still a weekly tradition in the Greek household for all the immediate and extended families to come together for lunch, usually at the parents' house.

The autumn sunshine was hot through the car window as the sun climbed higher in a cloudless sky. The damaged roads had narrowed somewhat between one village and the next, and we slowed down to almost a crawl to assess the situation. The road ahead had crumbled away, and a large part of it had fallen into the deep ravine below us. We looked across at several large boulders having been purposefully placed to act as temporary markers, indicating the new edge of a rapidly deteriorating road. As we cautiously proceeded, we noticed some thoughtful person had erected a few large bamboo sticks and placed them in an upright position into the gouged-out holes, with the addition of some plastic bottles being placed on top of the sticks to warn the motorist that this part of the road had also crumbled away!

Continuing along now, we left the dangerous hazard behind and listened to some Greek music on the local radio station, some pleasingly melodic stuff and some not too good. Pulling to the side of the road, Chris looked at the map to make sure we were heading in the correct direction. I saw an old donkey grazing on the verge outside a farmhouse and decided to get out and take a picture; he had an old traditional wooden saddle and harness, which is antique and not often seen. Putting my hand out to stroke his ears, the naughty thing lifted his head and pulled his lips back to try and bite me.

"Oh! I said in a loud voice, jumping back with shock; that's not very friendly. I only wanted to stroke you and take your picture; there's no need to bite me." I heard giggling coming from behind me; it was two little girls who had witnessed it all. I smiled and shrugged my shoulders with embarrassment before returning to the car.

Chris pointed to the two young girls and said, "They kept turning around and laughing at you; they must have known the donkey is bad-tempered and bites people."

On the road again, we marvel at the stunning beauty of the Cretan countryside, with the massive mountain ranges bathed in the warm autumn sunshine, throwing exquisite light and shade patterns over the undulating hills as the white scudding clouds drift by to temporarily block out the sun. Sometime later, we see a series of wispy low clouds drift lazily along, crossing the horizon on some other part of the mountain range.

"It looks like the angels have hung their washing out to dry," I whispered, trying to freeze-frame the wonderful views. It was just so beautiful not to stop and stare for a few minutes.

Parking the car inside a disused quarry we stood looking across at the changing colours on the mountainside; coupled with varying cloud formations, it made the overall view like a moving picture. We remarked about a house here on this spot and the privilege of looking at these views constantly.

"I'd never get any work done; I think I would just sit in the window and stare at the constantly changing beauty of it all."

This poem reminds me of that beautiful day;

What is this life if, full of care,
We have no time to stand and stare.
No time to stand beneath the boughs,
And stare as long as sheep or cows.
No time to see, when woods we pass,
Where squirrels hide their nuts in grass.
No time to see, in broad daylight,
Streams full of stars, like skies at night.
No time to turn at Beauty's glance,
And watch her feet, how they can dance.
No time to wait till her mouth can,
Enrich that smile, her eyes began.
A poor life this if, full of care,

By: William Henry Davies.

Back in the car and a few minutes later, we were approaching the tiny hamlet of Koufi. Passing a ruined house on our left, we saw the roof had completely collapsed in on itself with a large fig tree and an assortment of wild grasses and shrubs growing out in the centre. Further along, by the crumbling walls, we spotted a large wooden cross leaning against some jagged rocks on the corner edge of a small rocky path leading up from the road.

Always on the lookout for a new adventure, we were pulling our walking boots on and walking up the uneven path to see where it went. The wooden sign in neat Greek lettering indicated the shrine was called Agias Nikolaos. Steadily walking up the graduating slopes for two kilometres, there were a few well-rotted carcasses of dead goats which had been dumped by the side of the path. The smell was really bad in the hot afternoon sun, and we held our noses and quickly walked past them.

Further down, we came to another left turn which pointed the way to the little shrine, and nearby we saw something quite remarkable leaning against a stone wall; it was a crudely carved stone statue of a man about four feet high which looked to be predated Christian times. There was a lengthy description written in an old Greek script and carved on an olive wood plaque; we tried to read it but failed to do so. Eventually, the tiny dirt path edged itself along the top of a hillside with a deep ravine just below, leading up to the entrance gates of Agias Nikolaos. We entered through the gates and noticed several smooth large rocks; wedged in the rocks were icons of the Saint, along with personal gifts of tiny crosses, beads, flowers and photographs of loved ones who were ill or had passed away.

As we approached another overhang of rocks, we saw the tiny church of Agias Niklaos tucked away deep inside the cool interior of a cave; surrounding the front of the little shrine was some neatly carved stone seating covered with padded cushions for pilgrims to come and rest and pray. We sat down on the cushions and waited until a smiling young priest walked towards us with his hands outstretched, welcoming us to his lovely Holy place.

"*Yassas* (hello)," he said, shaking our hands. "My name is Father Yannis; what are your names?"

We introduced ourselves, and he replied, "Please sit down and rest awhile. Can I get you some coffee or water?" He picked up a beautiful carved stone bowl, sliding the heavy stone lid across, revealing some small chocolate biscuits inside; he told us one of his parishioners had taken the trouble to make it for him. He left us with our coffee and water and went over to his BBQ area to clean it before collecting some kindling wood from his little orange and lemon grove.

When we had finished our refreshments, we carefully opened the tiny doll's house door to the shrine's interior. Turning the old metal ring attached to the thick wooden door, weather-beaten over the centuries, we blinked to adjust our eyes from bright sunlight to the cool and gloomy interior, gasping in awe at one of the most opulent shrines we have seen so far. We couldn't step inside the shrine as it was so small; it would only hold one person – the Priest. We stood shoulder to shoulder gazing in at a large golden cross, some gold candlesticks, several ornate icons and pictures of Saints, including an icon of St George on his horse and slaying the dragon. He is the patron Saint of Greece as well as England; we know now St George was Greek, not English. Gently closing the door and nearby, we notice the ornate brass stand which holds a deposit of sand for worshippers to light their candles and say a prayer for loved ones.

Sometime later, we walked over to Father Yannis busily tending his BBQ; the dry kindling wood had caught well, producing some fierce flames, shooting up in the air. He told us his family was coming to share a meal with him later as it is Sunday. Chris asked him if he lived nearby, he pointed up to the top of the gorge, saying this was one shrine he took care of, but he preached and tended another four places of worship as well. I asked if we could take a look around his orange grove before leaving; he nodded and smiled as we walked up the steps and into a very well kept agricultural area. The narrow grove runs along the very edge of the gorge. We looked out over to the far side and down below onto the dense green canopy of trees, with a few deciduous trees already dressed in their autumn glory of gold, red and yellow leaves, giving a stark contrast to the vivid evergreen trees jostling amongst them on the valley floor. The migratory birds sweetly sang within the dense canopy of trees, and a light warm wind tickled our faces as we paused for a while to enjoy the peace and tranquillity. A deep sigh of contentment came from within as we took in the beautiful views; you could imagine a hermit living here as many others have all over the island and dedicate his life to prayer.

Returning to the shrine and Father Yannis, we warmly thanked him for his friendship and hospitality and shook hands once again. He remembered our names and wished us a safe onward journey. Father Yannis had mentioned an alternative path that led to an even better view of the gorge and thought we should try it. The day was still young, and we had plenty of time to visit the Tomb of the Five Virgins later in the day. The path became steeper as we descended, passing the back of a large overhang of rocks that housed the beautiful shrine of Agias Nikolas. Further along, an impressive limestone pavement came into view adjacent to an olive grove headed towards the top of the gorge walls; we paused to admire a field literally covered with huge limestone rocks with many large holes and fissures.

It looked a bit like a ruined village with caved-in walls, sunken paths and a lush overgrowth of wild shrubs and herbs. We continued our journey to join the top road; then, we had to give all our attention to the rapidly deteriorating path with all the lost rocks and stones; that was when I saw a mollusc, about half an inch in width. I bent down and picked it up, turning it over in my hand a few times; it was firmly ensconced in a piece of hard rock. A good example of a fossilised shell, almost intact and laid here so high on the top of the gorge walls and quite a few kilometres away from the sea. Reminding us again of when the tectonic plates shifted to fling the beautiful island of Crete out of the sea.

Returning from the circular walk, we saw Father Yannis's family get out of their cars and go to join him for lunch. There was the man and his wife with their three young children; then we realised that when we saw all the books and toys with a couple of slides and swings near the shrine, they were there to keep the children amused.

A quick check-up on the map, we drove towards the village of Argyroupoli, where its centre is dominated by lots of natural springs, constantly gushing clean drinking water from the many mouths of stone lion heads, along with ornate stone wells cascading down in large streams and waterfalls. The constant loud noise of mountain water fills the air as you enter the village. Very popular with tourists and locals alike, with a few fish restaurants displaying large tanks of live fish, including carp and bass, conveniently placed into the outside walls. The unique and interesting gift shops are situated around the village centre, tempting you to come in and take a look. A few other restaurants boast of very large outdoor BBQ areas where large automatic spits turn roasting goat or lamb; the aroma is mouth-watering and fills the air to tempt you to sample the succulent meat or dine on homegrown vegetables and salads. We see the local people coming with their large containers and fill them at the spring wells instead of using water at home; it is pleasing to always draw fresh, clean spring water all the year round.

We walked up to one of the elevated restaurants, boasting magnificent views over the village and beyond, to sit and rest awhile in the shade and have some lunch before moving on to our next destination.

Ancient Lapeon

Lapeon was a significantly powerful City. In Greek legend, it was believed to have been founded by the Greek hero Agamemnon. Argyroupoli is the present-day village built on the site of the ancient city with rich vegetation and natural water springs. A few beautiful Venetian mansions stand in various parts of the village, with some still occupied as homes. Many excavations have been undertaken in the area, revealing many beautiful artefacts, including a magnificent mosaic floor, Roman bathhouses and some interesting coins. Some twenty-four coins were minted in Lappa depicting Apollo, Poseidon, Diana and Athena. Some other twelve coins were dated from the Roman period depict various Roman Emperors. Many other finds include sculptures, statues, bone tools and pottery.

Pente Parthenes Church – The Tomb of the Five Saint Virgins

Situated a little way out of the village, the church was purposefully erected to the memory of the five Christian women who martyred themselves for defying the invading Romans around the third century and for secretly practising Christianity. They are buried in a vaulted Roman tomb just inside the church; their names were Thukela, Marianna, Athena, Martha and Maria.

We were just about to give up trying to find Ancient Lappa when I spotted a brown tourist sign indicating 'Ancient Lapeon and the Tomb of the Five Virgins'.

With walking boots on again, we followed the wayfarer sign pointing down a steep rocky track until it eventually petered out to give way to a smoother and much even stone walkway, obviously built and maintained during the Roman occupation. There were larger stones situated down the central walkway, with smaller partially shaped stones down each side to form a lovely herringbone pattern. Imagine the sandaled feet of the Romans tramping up and down the carefully constructed highways, along with a continual flow of many horses and wooden wheeled carts. We were walking in the footsteps of an ancient civilisation; it wasn't hard to visualise a busy Roman settlement here, with all the hustle and bustle of townsfolk going about their daily lives.

A little further along the splendid highway, we saw one of the stone cut funeral chambers which had been neatly gouged out in the rocks and etched with elaborate interior decoration; these were constructed by the Romans for their important dignitaries of the time. Eventually, we arrived at a little whitewashed church, taking its name from The Five Virgins, and when we opened the wooden door, a beautiful portrait of Jesus Christ gazed back at us within the gloomy interior. The artist had captured Jesus' loving kindness and compassion in his eyes, which appeared to follow us around the tiny circular room.

Slowly descending to the bottom of the valley, there is a magnificent 2,000-year-old plane tree standing majestically in its centre. The large spread of roots above ground was impressive. Tracing my forefinger along the gnarled and knotted bark, I looked up into the canopy of thick branches. They were fully extended to embrace the sky but bowed down under the extreme weight. We thought it would take about ten people, holding hands together, to circumvent the beautiful plane tree. Moving on again, we see some more deep-sided tombs etched out of the rock face; they appeared to be single tombs with a few double ones for man and wife. Some had deep stone niches where holy relics or personal items must have been placed near the body.

Wandering onto another visible track, running alongside a fast-flowing river, now swollen with a brief deluge of early autumn rain. An overgrowth of tall reeds and bamboo framed the riverbank and would have supplied the town with all the freshwater they would need. The tall reed grasses and sparse plane trees covered the lower banks as we walked, ankle-deep through crisp brown leaves shed by a variety of deciduous trees.

There were even more tombs on the other side of the valley, waiting for excavation with a dense tangle of hanging vines, wild shrubs and scrub grass growing in abundance.

This must have been quite a sizable town in its day, with much more to be uncovered.

We were delighted to have had such a wonderful experience, meeting Father Yannis and visiting the archaeological site of, The Tomb of the Five Virgins.

Chapter Twenty
Patsiano or Patsos Gorge

There had been strong winds and some rain during the night, constantly howling around our shuttered villa and waking us up with peals of thunder from time to time, thankfully it had 'blown' itself out, and we woke to a much better morning. Our friends who have the other villa nearby were coming with us to do a walk in The Patsos Gorge.

Driving through the beautiful countryside with the car windows open, we listen to the birds singing in the distance. The majestic Lefka Ori had another thin covering of freshly fallen snow, collecting in the crevices and fissures of the rock.

The beautiful, leafy Patsos Gorge, along with the tiny Agios Andonios cave shrine, was firstly Minoan and later Dorian, and then a Roman sanctuary. Etched out into a large overhang of rock and framed with a few wild trees and shrubs and so tiny, it holds only six people inside the beautiful interior. Agios Andonios or Saint Anthony is the Patron Saint of lost articles, and there you will see many lost or misplaced items just outside the door. Many little messages asking for prayer for loved ones have been written and wedged into tiny cracks in the rock next to the altar. Patsos Gorge is by far one of the most beautiful gorges we have seen on the island; it is very popular with the Cretan families who come on Sundays to have lunch in the large restaurant situated alongside the river, pouring down from the mountains above the gorge. For added interest, there is a small animal enclosure with donkeys for the children to ride as well as goats, rabbits and pigs; the last time we saw the pigs they had just finished eating left over spaghetti and had 'red moustaches' around their snouts!

Stopping for a while on the journey to Patsos, we stretched our legs and walked around some of the newly built Potamus Dam; they had flooded a whole village to erect the dam to collect fresh water for the local reservoir; it is an impressive feat of engineering. A small café overlooking the dam has recently been set up to cater for summer visitors. The Dam water is filled to the brim now from continual heavy rains during winter months, with many migratory birds nesting around the lake in the dense undergrowth to breed and hatch their youngsters.

On arrival at the Gorge, we found a parking space in the shade of an overhang of trees. Walking in through the gates, we passed several donkeys waiting to give the children a ride. At the head of the gorge and down a few cut stone steps, we stepped inside the lovely enclosure, which is Agios Andonios church. Once a year, on the Saints Name Day, there is a good festival here for everyone to come and worship and celebrate together. This sacred place was here long before the Christians and Craneos, Hermes was worshipped here until the fourth century A.D. Craneos comes from the word *krini,* which means spring and is pronounced *krana* in Doric dialect.

We have visited Patsos Gorge several times, at different times of the year, there is always something new and interesting to see. Today, we began the walk with our friends down the uneven rocky path and descended towards the bottom of the gorge, passing many boulders and the overhang of trees in the fast-flowing Patsos River. Bubbling and swirling over and around smooth rocks and boulders in the riverbed from the torrential snowmelt, cascading down throughout the year. Pretty little rock pools had formed between larger rocks, quite deep in parts but so clear, you could see the bottom of the river where so many little coloured stones, bright as tiny buttons, wink back at you in the afternoon sunlight. The gorge is approximately two metres long, rushing along its length towards the Potamus Dam before meandering its way to reach the Prasses Gorge some distance away, to continue its final journey into the swollen riverbeds at Platanes and out to sea.

Picking our way over rocks and boulders, occasionally swinging out around a firmly placed tree truck overhanging the river, we stop for a while to admire the tiny water-loving plants and ferns growing along the river bank. Other times of the year, we have seen little clusters of violets peeping up through emerald green ferns along with delicate white cyclamens growing up the bank sides. Climbing down again and leaving the little path for a while, we come across a fine sandbank situated up to the water's edge and watch the bright sunlight on the water casting light and shadow on the deep underbelly of a large boulder. My eyes travel from the boulder to an overhang of trees beyond; the sunlight shone through the rustling leaves in the warm breeze to send shards of light onto the constantly moving river.

It's all so beautiful and peaceful, freeing your soul; you close your eyes, slow down your breathing, listening to the steady tinkling sound of water and feel the warm wind and sun on your body. It's a time when you feel at peace with the world, and your cares and worries of the day slowly drift away, then you emit a sigh that comes from deep within. I truly believe this beautiful, wonderful island of Crete should be on prescription for everyone instead of taking tablets. We walked to where a large rock blocked our path; there was a metal ladder securely fixed to the massive boulder; you can climb down to continue walking down the gorge. Before the ladder was in place, there was just a thick rope attached to the top of the boulder, and climbers could abseil down to the next level; we did this the first time we visited Patsos Gorge a few years ago. This time we decided we were going to turn back and get something to eat in the shady restaurant and relax for a while.

In the doorway of the restaurant, there is a large parrot called Koko hopping about on his perch as we approached. I whistled to him a few times, but all I got for my trouble was a few croaking noises, so I gave up in the end. Just as we were walking away, Koko came out with a few Greek words which sounded very rude; we all turned around and laughed at him as the waiter came to greet us. Inside the cool, shady restaurant and along the wall, which is part of the gorge, was quite a lot of old photographs of the family as well as many others depicting resistant fighters and soldiers, which were taken during the Cretan Occupation. An eclectic mix of old Cretan memorabilia hung to one side of the doorway to the kitchen, old cooking pots and utensils, ancient gardening equipment, ploughs and *sakouli* (colourful woven cloth bags used in the mountains). At the far end of the restaurant, there is a large domed spit outside, roasting succulent lamb and goat meat for the table. This opens out to an immaculate grassy area where children can play with some swings and slides over to the right. A small garden had been made by the family, growing many local herbs and flowers, and each one had a label to say what they were. The restaurant itself is very large and caters on a regular basis for Birthday celebrations and Wedding Parties. It is normal for Cretan families to invite 1,000 or even three to 4,000 people to a Wedding Reception. Personally, we don't know a hundred people let alone that amount, but it is usually Cretan friends of friends, and the list goes on. We have been to a Christening; it was considered a small affair of three hundred or so.

The Greek people love to party as much as they love their food and drink, meeting up with their friends and family in the afternoon or evenings, when the day has cooled down. It's not only the adults who come out in the evenings the children and babies come along too; we have seen several generations of the same family sitting together at a large table filled with food, enjoying themselves for a few hours and celebrating life!

In the restaurant today, we see large trestle tables down the length of the room with families of 20 or more sitting together, several generations from babies to great grandparents – talking, eating, laughing and enjoying themselves; it's lovely to see and reminds you of how families should be with each other.

Paradi And Kelter On The Psiloritis Mountains

There is always so much to see and so much to do on this beautiful island, so it came as no surprise to us when we get enticed and re-directed to visit other places of interest on our day out.

This happened one day when we were coming back from a day's walking in the mountains. Driving through the sleepy village of Nithavri I noticed a rusty road sign indicating the way to Pardi and Kelter leading up to a walking shelter at the top. As it was mid-afternoon, we decided to take a look and check it out for possible walking in the future.

We had the Vitari 4x4 which made driving on the bumpy uneven track a lot easier. Magnificent views instantly opened up to us as we began to climb up towards a large natural cave on our left and sheep shelter to our right. The air was so pure and clean as I stopped to open the double gates, these are closed later in the year when the snow comes as it is dangerous to proceed. Eventually we came to a stop outside a tiny church, Agios Titos and looked inside to admire the interior.

On the undulating mountainside was a dense woodland of 'stunted' oak trees, continually battered by the harsh elements down the centuries. Their gnarled trunks and branches reaching out in a haphazard fashion and their sharp tiny leaves were half the size of normal oaks. A thick carpet of previously shed acorns littered the ground beneath the trees, a sure sign no squirrels resided there.

We did go back the following year and the year after that to climb the Psiloritis in stages, each time we left a prominent stone 'cairn' to remind us to begin the next part of the walk until we reached the top. We were lucky one day when we're gazing down a gully and the magnificent views across to the south coast when we heard a whooshing sound coming from behind us. A large bird of prey swooped past us, intent on catching his quarry. We could feel the draught from his wings, then he neatly folded them tightly against his body to gather maximum speed.

"Wow, oh wow!" I exclaimed, getting really excited. "How lucky are we to see that, nature in the raw!" I added.

During the time of Minoans much of Crete had large areas of woodland, but over time a lot of the forests were systematically cut down to build wooden ships for sea-fairing and trade. They had the biggest navy at that time. It took two thousand trees to make just one sailing ship.

Askifou Plateau and Around

2nd Week in November

The last flight out of Heraklion, usually the second week of November, although there are a few flights during the winter months which can be expensive, flying via Athens and then to Crete. Usually, we leave Crete and fly back to England for the winter months, then come back for their Easter in April. Greek Easter is a moveable feast, altering each year slightly and usually a week ahead or just after England's, so if we time it right, we can enjoy two Easter celebrations.

A few years ago, we were coming back from good days walking in the mountains and passing through the village of Askifou Sfakia – a series of little mountain villages running in close proximity to the White Mountains on our left. I saw a signpost indicating a WW2 War Museum and thought we should stop and take a look. War Museums are not everyone's 'cup of tea', but the vast collection inside the old building and outside was amazing. Outside the museum, there were aeroplane propellers, a Norton motorbike captured by the Germans from the Allies, then put to work for the invading forces, armoured tanks, hastily abandoned by the Germans when they fled the island. A nice young lady greeted us at the door of the museum in well-spoken English; she said that she was the third generation of her grandfather Yiorgos Hatzidakis who witnessed the German invasion as a child here in the village. She showed us inside the large room; it is an impressive assortment of photographs, helmets, badges and weapons, magazines and posters, and these were all in separate sections depending on the Nationality. We spent an interesting two hours browsing at the fascinating collection before being offered some raki and biscuits. The museum stays open on donations from the public and with no financial help from the Greek government, which we thought was such a shame. The collection is continually being expanded, with people bring various pieces of WW2 memorabilia.

The private museum covers all countries concerned in the occupation of Crete in 1941. Greece, England, New Zealand, Australia, Germany. You can get more information on the internet by typing in 'Askifou Museum'. You will see many photographs and memorabilia of the huge collection, there may also be the opening times because the young lady lives across the road from the museum, so I don't think it will be a problem to visit the museum.

Asi Gonia Village, Home of George Psychoundakis, 'The Cretan Runner'

Our last adventure of the year took us up to Asi Gonia in the White Mountains for the day with our friends, Chrissie and Jacqui. We had all read The Cretan Runner, faithfully re-written by Sir Patrick Lee Fermor, taken from George's diary when he did many brave wartime treks in the mountains, carrying messages to intelligence outposts in a bid to win the war over the German occupation of 1941. Arriving in the quiet sleepy mountain village mid-morning, we looked around the village square for a bronze memorial of George, but there wasn't anything there to mark his bravery, only a bust of Venizelou and associated heroes.

Beyond Asi Gonia, we followed the rapidly deteriorating road leading to the village of Kalikratis, climbing steadily and rocky and broken in parts with narrow and sharp hairpin bends; we go from laughing and chatting to a deep pregnant silence. Turning around to look at Jacqui, she had turned pale and had her hand over her eyes to avoid looking down on the sheer drop into the gorge below. It didn't get any better the further we climbed, and on a broad left-hand bend, we decided to turn back.

It was Chrissie who spotted the wooden sign first – George Psychoundakis Museum. When we got out of the car, we noticed the double doors of the museum were closed and locked but nearby was a middle-aged man and woman working in the field next to the building. They came over and introduced themselves. "I am Nikos, George Psychoundakis, son, and this is my wife," he said smiling. We were all astonished; we didn't know George P. had any family.

"Please, come in and look inside my father's house", he added. The house inside was traditional and beautiful. He said, "It was built by my father when he and his sister were very young." There were many old photographs displayed inside the house, many black and white photos of George with the resistance fighters, along with certificates of acknowledgement from the Greek government for his part in the occupation, as well as an audience with Queen Elizabeth of England and several other warm acclamations from various institutes in Crete and abroad.

Nikos points to a photograph of his father with all his brothers and sisters. We were standing in a part of the house which had been extended; he then led us to the older original part with a very low ceiling held up by some big wooden beams. We had to stoop low to go inside; this was the sitting room – very comfortable with a wooden high back couch covered in a brightly coloured throw. The thick stone walls were almost covered with more pictures of George depicting his colourful life and his achievements. Nikos drew our attention to the wooden ladders just behind the couch, which led up to George's bedroom.

We were invited to sit and drink some raki and a snack with Nikos and his wife and talked about his father's life. He asked us if we would like to come to the local graveyard in the village where George and his wife Maria were buried. It was very moving, and Nikos shed a tear as we paid our respects to a legend, a brave man who will never be forgotten. George was 85 years old when he died in 2006.

This memorable day turned out to be the last adventure of the year; we would be flying home for the winter in two days. We would be busy preparing the villa, packing things away and covering the furniture up, as well as saying goodbye to all our lovely friends we have come to know and love.